SR

Earthy Mysticism

William McNamara

EARTHY MYSTICISM

Contemplation and the
Life of Passionate Presence

CROSSROAD · NEW YORK

I wish to express my appreciation to Tessa Bielecki,
without whose dedication an editorial expertise
this book would not have been possible.

1984
The Crossroad Publishing Company
370 Lexington Avenue, New York, NY 10017

Library of Congress Cataloging in Publication Data

McNamara; William.
Earthy mysticism.

1. Spiritual life—Catholic authors.
2. Contemplation.   3. Prayer.   I. Title.
BX2350.2.M385 1983   248.2′2   82-23554
ISBN 0-8245-0562-X (pbk.)

TO FATHER DAVID SAMUEL LEVIN,
a Jewish earthy mystic of the Nada Community,
Crestone, Colorado

> May a singular passion sweep over me like a tidal wave, quickening every fiber of my body, stirring my soul to the depths, bringing together and to a boil all my emotional energy, and marshalling all the forces of my erotic being into an intellectual act of unconditional and universal love of God. May nothing of me or the scabrously raw matter of my being-in-the-world be left out of this vast and undivided love. Amen.
>
> *William McNamara*

ACKNOWLEDGMENTS

Excerpt from page 24 from CRIME AND PUNISHMENT by Fyodor Dostoevsky, translated by Constance Garnett. Used by permission of Random House, Inc.

Excerpt from page 320 of the "Epilogue" to THE DEVILS OF LOUDUN by Aldous Huxley. Copyright 1952, by Aldous Huxley. By permisson of Harper & Row Publishers, Inc.

Excerpt from THE MYTH OF THE GREAT SECRET by E. Clark Johnson. Used by permission of William Morrow and Company, Inc.

"The Birth of the Outlaw Church" first appeared as "The Desert Experience and the Birth of the Outlaw Church" in the May, 1980 issue of *Studies in Formative Spirituality*.

"The Birth of the Outlaw Church" first appeared as "Spirituality and the Desert Experience" in *Studies in Formative Spirituality*, Vol. I., No. 2 (May, 1980). Used by permission.

Contents

Introduction

T he mystic is not a special kind of person; every person is a special kind of mystic. The mystic is one who consciously and thoroughly immerses himself in the mystery of life and enjoys communion with ultimate Being. Everyone is partially immersed in the mystery, and to some small degree, enjoys communion with ultimate Being. The mystic knows God by experience—not by periodic and dramatic peak experiences, but by the unremarkable, quotidian experience of a lifetime. Little by little, quite imperceptibly, the Spirit of God seeps in and takes possession of the mystic. The same Holy Spirit that Christened Jesus in one way, Christens the mystic in another. While this happens to the great mystics in an obvious and unmistakable way, it happens to the rest of us—or at least it can—in a pedestrian way.

The authentic Christian mystic is notoriously earthy. He loves the earth and takes good care of it. He remains as poor as possible so that he can leave many earthly things unused, and therefore unspoiled by human greed. He recognizes how sacramental the earth is. In this he resembles the North American Indian. He works on the earth in a leisurely way in order to be a good, practical steward and a reverent contemplative instead of a rapacious consumer. He enjoys the earth and finds his delight in it, without being inordinately attached to it. He knows he is in exile on earth; but he also knows that his exile is erotic, so he makes the most of it: he

sees everything as a sign, sample or symbol of God and therefore he affirms the totality of being, celebrates chastely, and
moves on obediently, restless until he rests in God.

The pain of an erotic exile does not escape him. Like Teresa of Avila, he considers his earthly existence as "a night in
a bad inn." But, again, like Teresa, he makes the most of it.
He copes creatively with the exigencies of life, solving most
problems humorously and living with unresolved problems
good-naturedly. During the mystic's exile, God comes and
goes. Though he suffers the Beloved's absence enormously,
he bears it quietly and expectedly. Far more than Peter, he
feels he can pray with utter sincerity: "Depart from me, O
Lord, for I am a sinful man" (Luke 5:9). But that one visi-
tation, that elusive presence, that passing touch, and, therefore, that wound, is enough to keep him alive forever—but
unsatisfied and unfulfilled until God comes and brings to
fruition the final love affair. Naturally, in the *mean*time—and
there *is* something "mean" about it—he will watch and wait
with heightened anticipation; he will suffer the mounting
paroxysm of terror and delight, not mincingly or fatuously, but
joyfully. There will be, undoubtedly, an awesome dénouement. After all, each unique and unrepeatable life is a drama,
not merely a process. And in each case the drama is inescapably tragic and comic. Tragic, because how can a disciple of
Jesus escape what the Master himself could not escape: suffering, rejection and crucifixion? And comic, because of the
unforeseeable in every life, the serendipities that are always
such a preposterously pleasant surprise.

Because of this miraculous dimension of life—the God connection—which reaches its peak in suffering (not the cure of
suffering), all kinds of broken, wounded lives are bearable;
not only bearable, but capable of healing and transformation.
We don't need to be saved from suffering. Suffering is an
earthy perennial, a Christian imperative. There is nothing
morbid about the earthy mystic, no limp resignation. He

is no ninny, no little lamb. He faces disgrace and death in the leonine manner of Christ, who was deceptively meek and disarmingly mighty. The earthy mystic needs to be Zorbatic and Aslanic enough to forget himself and follow, with pride and panache, the Suffering Servant all the way. He intends to suffer so well that he will break through to resurrection. And since the final breakthrough takes forever, he never measures or calculates his suffering. Nor does he try to skirt death. The wound is healed and the promise kept only on the other side of death. No wonder all the robust romantics felt exactly the same way St. Teresa and St. John of the Cross did, when their poetry used the very same phrase to express their poignant prayerful passion: "I die because I cannot die."

Finally and simply, the Christian must be mystical because Christ was perfectly mystical and he must be earthy because Christ was—and is—the earthiest person on earth.

NOTE: Even the lowliest of earthy mystics cherishes the languages of earth and refuses to do violence to his own language, and so, despite footling fads and popular pressures, he will never resort to awkward, messy, linguistic devises such as "(s)he," "he or she," or "woperson," when a simple "he" or "person" will do the trick. Any truly liberated woman will understand this policy.

CHAPTER 1

God in the Flesh

Western mysticism is necessarily an earthy mysticism. The source of Christian mysticism is in the earth, in the world, in the flesh. To say this is not to speak of confinement but of contentment. This is marvelously true in two senses. First of all, God has revealed that he is contented to dwell in us and that he finds his delight in us when we embody him. And when we enflesh him *consciously* and *creatively*, there is no end to his delight. It is as unconfined as an active volcano. In a second sense, there is divine contentment in the human venture. If we are ever to cross over without delay or anxiety, if we are ever going to enjoy the "passover," then our sole content, as wayfarers and pilgrims of the Absolute, must be divine; that is to say, we must be God-centered human beings, earthy enfleshments of the Numinous.[1]

God in the flesh means God in the heart. Keep this in mind when I begin to talk about prayer as a cry of the heart. Whose prayer do we hear in the Alleluia Chorus and the wailing at the wall, in the scream from the bed and the howl from the cross? At the heart of hearts is the cry. It is the source of all music and all gladness, all joy and all sadness. To learn to be in tune with that cry and then to intone it with all of one's heart and all of one's breath—this is what it means to live.

The cry that summons us into being, into life, into undreamed of realms of love, is the eternal, infinite reality that the New Testament refers to as "the Word." St. John says, "In the beginning was the Word . . . and the Word was made flesh" (John 1:1, 14). The Word was made flesh originally, not in the age of Augustus Caesar, but in the beginning. The Incarnation did not begin with Christmas but with creation. The Incarnation reached its peak in Jesus who expressed the Word, verbally and bodily, with such a degree of amplitude that no Christology has been able to fit "this man" into our human possibilities or mental categories.

The flesh that God became in the beginning was raw matter, cosmic material, the stuff of the universe. It is highly significant that tradition has always associated the Word or the Logos with the original act of creation: the act of God, which goes on and on. At the heart of everything is the supreme initiative of the One who acts, the One who is always there. At work and at leisure, he is there. On each of the six days of creation, he is there. And on the seventh, he is there. History is the story of how humans became cocreators. And we will continue to be cocreators, builders of the Kingdom, until the One who in the beginning chose to dwell in us will come again, reassert his sovereign claim, and gather all the fragmented and estranged shreds of being into the reconciled opposites of the one Word. As St. John of the Cross said, from all eternity God speaks one word; nothing remains to be said.

God does not act in a vacuum. The word resounds in us. We bring to the cry of God a little fulfillment. And to the degree we do that, we bring on the Parousia. As the Word resonates in us, the mystery of Faith unfolds, the enfleshment of God increases. This enfleshment provides for us a focus of what would otherwise be invisible and unbearable. Such incredible becomings: the divine becoming human, the infinite becoming finite, the spiritual becoming material, and the eternal becoming subject to time and space. The Word reached its finest focus in Jesus. It will reach its final expression in the Parousia. We live between the focus and the fulfillment. It is by coping creatively with the exigencies of life that we engage in the perpetual and progressive enfleshment of God. The Creator has entrusted himself to creation, to our freedom. He is always there, pure Spirit, longing to be enfleshed.

What God requires of us is trustful cooperation through creative activity. The Kingdom has been handed over to us. We are entrusted with God and his world, with the totality of being. God and man are involved, mutually, in self-actualizing surrender. We trust him who trusts us with the future of the planet and the well-being of our neighbor. Once we replace this trustful and grateful allegiance to God with a fearful, tight grip on our own homemade egos, the activities of life take a destructive turn. Our interpersonal and international relationships are so chaotic because we are so unrelated to the ultimately real: God in us, the Word made flesh. There is no human peace without divine communion.

In order to engage in truly creative activity, we must learn to unite contemplation and action. Action without contemplation is blind. When we are driven into feverish activity, activity that is not inspired and empowered by contemplation, we do more harm than good. Our busyness enslaves us. Those who succeed us will be even busier and more encumbered. They will be forced to undo all that we have done, because our work was not inspired by the Holy Spirit and, therefore, did not prepare the way for the processive enfleshment of the Logos.

What characterizes the harmonious activity of human beings that we call creative activity is *stillness*, the stillness in the cat ready to pounce, the stillness of an artist at work, the stillness of an army ready for attack. The stillness of creative activity is very different from a flaccid, limp kind of relaxation. At the end of our common morning prayer at Nova Nada, we pray this Shaker prayer: "Now is the time to be still. And we will." In the evening we enjoy a relaxed kind of stillness and quietude, but our mornings are characterized by a creative, forceful, unpredictable kind of stillness that leads us, we hope, through active contemplation into creative activity. If God so pleases, we are led beyond creative activity into passive contemplation. But we must first be responsible ourselves for an active kind of contemplation that leads desirably into creative activity, because creative activity is the realm of the enfleshed Logos.

Only a free person is capable of creative activity and so, ultimately, capable of God. Freedom does not mean doing anything you want to do. It means really wanting to do what you must do to open up all the taut teguments of the flesh to the power of the Spirit. Jesus was so utterly free and thus so thoroughly inbred with the divine love that he became the Christ. In this definitive dénouement of the Word made flesh, God reconciled all things to himself. The Church, the body of Christ, continues this reconciliation by prolonging and extending the enfleshment of the Word into the farthest reaches of the world.

In the Church the Eucharist plays a central role. Every Eucharist *remembers* Jesus. Understand that the word *remembers* is precisely the opposite of *dismembers*. At every Eucharist the body of Christ takes a visible shape. During the priestly memorial action of the Church, because of the presence and the power of its head, pieces of cosmic material, bread and wine, bearing the marks of human industry and creative activity, become capable of mediating to people the vitality of Christ in a particularly powerful way. The consecrated bread and wine focus with special sharpness the wider reality I am trying to highlight at this time: the enfleshment of God in all flesh. The Eucharist is a celebration of this marvelous mystery as well as a focused embodiment of it. This enfleshment means that the Word is as much a part of the universe as the hydrogen atom. Like Christ and the Church, the Eucharist is a focus of the enfleshed Word. It is not a closed event but open-ended and outward-looking. The intrinsic dynamism of the Eucharist extends infinitely beyond the boundaries of the liturgy and the liturgical actions of the Church. We must recognize this link between liturgy and life, between worship and work. Otherwise we become stultified and disgrace the universal Church.

There are three dramatic and practical implications of the enfleshed Logos. First, there is no such thing as divine intervention. How can a transcendent God who is simultaneously immanent, who is already operating through the Logos from within the entire universe, come from or act from without? Ordinarily the Incarnation is designated as the finest example of intervention. Not so. The Incarnation is simply the supreme focus. Another implication of the enfleshed Logos is that there is no separation between the transcendent God and the material word; there is no careful demarcation between the sacred and the secular. We still need specially sacred places and specially sacred times. But there is no dichotomy between the sacred and the profane.

Finally, if the enfleshment of the Logos is perpetual, progressive and universal, the spiritual is not necessarily superior to the material. The material *is* spiritual. We must acknowledge that there is human activity that is destructive and therefore not possibly within the realm of the enfleshed Logos. This destructive human activity opposes the creative activity of the enfleshed Logos and is called evil. As we take a strong stand against evil, we push back the barriers and extend the domain of the enfleshed Logos.

Thus, enfleshed Logos has a fourfold focus: Christ, the

Church, the Eucharist and the Consecration. The Eucharist
is the event where the faithful gather together and provide a
visible, tangible, palpable example and embodiment of the
Church, and the Consecration comprises the central dominical words and actions of the liturgy by which the bread and
wine become the body and blood of Christ. So, you have the
incarnate Word containing Christ, Christ containing the
Church, the Church containing the Eucharist, and the Eucharist containing the Consecration. It is important to note
that this order of things cannot be reversed: Christ does not
contain or confine the enfleshed Word of God; the Church
does not contain Christ; the Eucharist does not contain or
constrict the Church; and the Consecration itself is so dynamic that it bursts the boundaries of the Eucharistic celebration, touching and uplifting the whole world.

Only now do I dare say something about Christmas. What
I have to say is not very different from what Bishop John A.
Robinson said over twenty years ago when we worked to-
gether at Esalen in California. What does Christmas teach us?
The mystery of Christmas claims that in that Baby and the
Man who grew from him is to be found the clue to the mean-
ing of all life. The Christmas Gospel, the "Good News" of
Christmas, the "tidings of great joy," reveal that what we see
in Jesus tells us more about the heart of the universe than
anything else.

Regardless of what we see on the surface of life, however
absurd, ridiculous, shallow, superficial, or mundane, at the
bottom of it all we discover what Christ looks like, sounds
like, is. That is why it is so important to get to the bottom
of the mystery of all mysteries, to the bottom of the universe,
to the rock bottom that is love, upon which the whole universe is constructed.

There is a common trait in all of mankind, humankind if
you will, and that is the invincible cupidity for the callipy-

gian dimension of other human beings! This is a symptom and a symbol of an even deeper drive, a deeper cupidity, a deeper need: to understand and to fathom the very bottom of the world.

What is at the bottom of the Christmas story? It is that love of the quality embodied in Christ is the most real, the most important thing in the world. Christmas claims that Jesus of Nazareth is the deepest probe into the meaning of everything. For in him we reach rock bottom, and there is no other. What we see on the surface is history. But in Jesus we see what lies at the center. In Jesus, the reality of the whole work, of the whole universe, breaks through.

The naked truth of Christ, the unalloyed, unequivocal reality of Christ enthralled the writers of the New Testament. They wanted to convey the ultimate significance of Christ, who was so astonishing, so absolutely unselfish, that you could see right through him as through a window into the Godhead. God was in Christ! Christ was in fact the God-man! This is the central proclamation of the New Testament writers. Because they were men of their age—a super-naturalist age—they indicated this divinity of Christ in the only way they knew how: with a glint of glory, a flutter of wings and a display of sheer miracle.

But today the poetry, imagery and magic of Christmas has lost its effect on almost everyone. Instead of increasing our dose of reality to the point where it hurts and heals, the traditional poetry, imagery, and magic of Christmas dilutes the message and dims the lights of revelation. Christmas has escaped us. It is infinitely worth stripping Christmas down to its bare essentials and paying close attention to the unbearable reality of the mystery itself. Not the language of the mystery, not the stories, the titles, the poetry, the imagery, but the *mystery itself*, a mystery which is—without the grace of God—wholly unbearable.

At Christmastime we do not merely commemorate Jesus. We celebrate the increasingly good news that God is indeed with us. With this brand new Christ-focus we learn how to enjoy the perpetual, progressive, and universal enfleshment of the Logos.

One final question, a Christmas question: Is Christ unique because he is abnormal or is he unique because he is normal? The Gospel claims that in this man we see the uniquely normal human being, the one who alone was what all of us were meant to be, free men—free from self and all the encroachments of grasping, craving ego, therefore free for all the others, through all the others free to worship, serve, and enjoy God as he is in himself.

Christmas, the Incarnation, is the end of the seventh day. Not end as closure but end as inevitable unfoldment. To understand this we must side with Dun Scotus rather than Thomas Aquinas. God came principally because he wanted to, secondarily because we needed him. It was his joy, his delight, his pleasure, his passion: to be with man. The Incarnation was therefore intrinsic to the original act of creation. It has to be.

On the seventh day God saw that his creation was good. And he blessed it with his personal delighted presence. By doing that, he paved the way for his coming in the Incarnation. An old catechism holds that our reason for existence is to enjoy God forever. The Gospel message is that God had the same idea. He came to enjoy us forever. As I shall repeat very often in this book, the Kingdom of God is the Kingdom of his coming. He comes, not "at the drop of a hat," but through every crack of the flesh. The hardened shell of the flesh is cracked open by every self-sacrificing, God-glorifying act of human love. Only a wild, ego-denying love-life can make way for his coming—the coming of Christ, who, as Thomas Merton says, now sleeps in our paper flesh like dynamite.

NOTES

1. That is why, though it is a heartbreaking experience to leave Sedona, Arizona, our original eremitical foundation, it is thrilling to move to the mountain wilderness of a state (Crestone, Colorado) whose motto is *Nil sine Numine:* "Nothing without God." What an appropriate place for Nada (the name of our monastic community), which means "nothing."

CHAPTER 2

Sensuous Prayer

> To pray, to pray that a whole people be spared from
> falling among the dead souls, the dead peoples, the dead
> nations, be spared from falling down dead, be spared
> from becoming a dead people, a dead nation, be spared
> from mildew, be spared from going rotten in spiritual
> death, in the earth, in hell.
>
> *Charles Péguy*

I would love to see Péguy's quotation emblazoned on every house of prayer, every monastery, convent and church, wherever people pray—as an antidote to our smooth tendency to pray softly and pray easily, in a dull, selfish, stultified, insular way, a sleepy kind of prayer. In his book on Joan of Arc, Péguy goes on and on and you sense the anguish and desperation in his words. The words do not slip easily from his lips and are wrung from the heart of one who sweats great drops of blood falling down to the ground.

Prayer is a terrible good. There is a terrible urgency about it, a mightiness, an awfulness. Prayer is sapiential, not soporific. We must make this distinction because of a general pervasive tendency among the best people, among the most impressive experts, to talk about prayer almost exclusively in terms of a soporific act, "a sleep of the faculties." That description of prayer comes from the great classics: John of the Cross, Teresa of Avila, *The Cloud of Unknowing*. But it can be easily misunderstood.

There is a world of difference between what is sapiential and what is soporific. They are opposite poles. Sapiential literally means having "a taste for the right things." The way toward this enjoyment of the right things is through taste, through touch, through the eyes and the ears and all of the senses; in other words, through a sensuous experience of life. Prayer is sapiential, not soporific. There is nothing more evident in the Gospel. Jesus constantly speaks of prayer in terms of attending to things, in terms of watchfulness. He seldom speaks of prayer alone but rather, "Watch and pray" (Matt. 26:38). What destroys his equilibrium and depresses him is that even after a long period of training, his disciples are not alert enough, not awake enough, not watchful enough, and, therefore, not prayerful enough, not intuitive enough, not in tune with the Father and the Father's world.

G. I. Gurdjieff, a recent philosopher-theologian, developed his whole spirituality on the concept of watchfulness as opposed to the soporific, as opposed to sleepiness. He says that the whole world of humanity is too sleepy and too passive. We must be *wisely* passive, which is *sapiential*. The goal of all education, all religion and all discipline is wise passiveness. Instead, we are *simply* passive, letting too many things happen to us, allowing our faculties to go to sleep without first having developed them. There is no way to become sufficiently intellectual and educated without first becoming sensuous. Hosea says: "Take some words and turn to the Lord" (Hos. 14:3). In a book on prayer, Allen Eccleston suggests that we turn to the Lord with two words: *engagement* and *passion*. These two finely chosen words characterize prayer.

Engagement—to be wholly, totally, fascinatingly, captivatingly engaged by God and therefore simultaneously by humanity, by the social, political world. We cannot go to prayer without the world. There is no such thing as *private prayer*. *Private prayer* is an anomaly, a contradiction, an impossibility. There is *solitary* prayer, but only because of our *solidarity* with the universe, with the earth, with people. In solitary prayer we become high priests of creation and accept our responsibility for the world. We must not dare ever to come into the aweful presence of God alone. God will say, "Where are the others? Where is my broken world? Where is that torn humanity for which my son died? Where is your anxiety? Have you wept enough? Have you sweated enough? Have you really prayed the way Péguy suggests we pray?" We need to be thoroughly, totally engaged—not unengaged, not withdrawn, not simply passive, not sleepy, not soporific, but sapiential. Eccleston also suggests that our engagement be carried out passionately. We can't be passionately engaged and sleep!

One great teacher I recently heard suggested that the best times for prayer are the sleepiest times, when we are most tired, because we slip right into a soporific condition of mind and God takes over. That may be true. That is a valid way of speaking of a certain *limited* form of prayer. There are some times when we can glorify God in our sleepy state of mind. But it is nothing to strive for! St. Thérèse of Lisieux justified her sleep in prayer by saying, "Maybe God loves me more asleep!" If that was true of Thérèse, it is probably eminently true of us! We are so cantankerous, so talkative, gregarious, loquacious: only if God puts us to sleep may he take over. In that sense—accidentally and periodically—soporific prayer may be a good form, but it is not the kind of prayer we should aspire to.

Many speakers on prayer today suggest that we make a concentrated, direct effort to put the faculties to sleep. Insofar as this is done we are moving toward a subrational human condition. And that is not prayer. That subrational human condition, that dehumanized state of mind, may resemble prayer, but it is not prayer. Prayer—by the grace of God—is the opposite. Instead of sinking down into a subrational condition by deliberately letting the faculties go to sleep, the truly prayerful person activates his senses to the highest possible degree until they become so saturated, so filled, so highly developed, that there is nothing more they can do. Then he breaks the bounds of the merely human mechanisms of knowing and loving and leaps into the void. Then there is a communication with God from the very ground of our being, from the origin, from the source.

We do not reach the source of being, the ground of our being, by recession, regression, withdrawal, or a diminution of human powers but by the fulfillment of our human powers, by the activation of the senses and the faculties: sensing as much as we can sense, feeling as much as we can feel, knowing as much as we can know. Then, convinced that this world and our little minds cannot possess God, we are drawn by the power of the Spirit into a *soirée* way beyond the realm of the faculties, through the night, into the banquet, into God himself. That is sapiential prayer.

En route to this stillness, this quietude, this emptiness, this serenity and tranquility, which we do not set up for ourselves but are given, prayer takes many forms. In the Judaeo-Christian tradition, one dominant form of prayer is turmoil, fury, frenzy, excitement, stimulation. The great old prophets and the great old mystics argued with God, fulminated with God, fumed with God, wept in his presence, laughed in his presence. They did not go to sleep. And if they did, God or Christ—his embodiment—was vastly offended. "Watch and pray." Attentiveness, watchfulness, alertness, sagacity—these are the characteristics of prayer until God himself stills us.

Our trouble lies in our superficial exposure to the classics. We read St. John of the Cross, Teresa, and *The Cloud of Unknowing*. We say, "The ultimate realm of prayer is stillness." We believe we should stop all our thinking, all our talking, our wishing, our desiring and let God speak, let God act. Yes, true enough. But as Picasso said: "It takes a long time to become young." What we are after is rebirth. It takes a long time to be reborn. It takes forever. It takes the longest imaginable discipline of life to be born into this instant. We cannot slip into it. We've got to develop. We've got to grow. That development and that growth involve numerous expressions of prayer. We see this magnificently portrayed in the mystics and the prophets—the real men and women of prayer.

We should engage in two very specific forms of prayer: morning and evening. Morning prayer should be very different from our evening prayer. Very often evening prayer rightfully takes the shape of prayer that people influenced either by the Orient or by *The Cloud of Unknowing* suggest. In the evening we have worked a whole day. We have lived a whole day. If we have really lived it with all we've got, then we are bound to be tired and exhausted by five o'clock. So evening prayer should be a quiet, largely passive, tranquil, serene period during which we are refreshed, reinvigorated and recharged by being in touch with our own center with few words, few concepts, few ideas, few images. We should simply be there, bathed in the fulgent presence of God, enlightened by him, and by him remade. In the evening this seems ideal.

But not in the morning. Most normal people have slept all night—some as long as six or seven hours! We do not need more sleep or a similar form of refreshment. Morning prayer should not be Teresian but Ignatian, not Oriental but Western, not passive but extremely active and athletic. In the morning we take hold of the day, so our prayer should be most watchful, most attentive, stimulating, exciting, full of aspiration, expectation and resolution. We should be jumping around on our chairs, hopping up and down, looking out the window! All these are signs that something is going on. Something *should* go on at morning prayer: brand new ideas, brand new aspirations, a brand new way of coping with this brand new day and this life.

Evening prayer should be more contemplative, but morning prayer should be more meditative, more thoughtful. One question, for instance, might be raised: "Who am I?", an age-old basic fundamental meditation. In this particular meditation you trace all the developmental stages that led to you. In examining those developmental stages—from the amoeba to you, from the worm to you, from the ape to you—you embrace and draw into your unique, distinct, magnificent, incredibly wonderful being all that was, all that is. You are overwhelmed by your dignity, by your nobility, your uniqueness. Then you still must say, "I am relatively nothing." The plentitude of being leads you to your contingency, your utter dependence upon God.

This reflection on matter, on history, on geography, on anthropology, leads you into God—the real God, not a surrogate god, not a makeshift god. God is a spendthrift who will squander you once you let him. But it's got to be *you* he squanders; not an undeveloped you, not an unrefined you, not a half-developed you, not a half-activated you, not a sleepy you, not a soporific you, but a *fully developed* you.

CHAPTER 3

Prayer in the City

A group of city sophisticates asked Giles, the Swiss hermit, what it was like to pray. They probably expected an esoteric answer. But he swept them off their feet when he said: "Prayer is like going off to dance or to war."

It doesn't make any difference whether you live in the desert or the city—prayer is the same: a cry of the heart. The point is *to live*. If you live wholeheartedly you will pray. That is why you cannot schedule prayer or contrive it. You can say your prayers, you can meditate, you can perform liturgical acts, but if these orations, meditations, and rituals do not express the reality of a life lived with such ardor that the heart is broken wide open, then there is no prayer. What is frequently mistaken for prayer is either pious prattle or a very proper preparation for prayer. There is no such thing as a casual cry of the heart. You cannot slip into prayer. I often see announcements that read: "Spontaneous prayer this afternoon between two and three pm." How can spontaneous prayer be scheduled? In Brian Moore's *Catholics*, the haunting story of a man's search for faith in a faithless world, the Abbot makes a final, crucial statement to his monks: "Prayer is the only miracle. We pray. If our words become prayer, God will come."

"It is a terrible thing to be caught in the hands of the living God" (Heb. 10:31). Every time you pray you enter into the cave of a lion. You should not count on a safe exit. Therefore, be slow to pray. Be sure to pray. But do not pray lightheartedly or frivolously. Do not trivialize God.

"The beginning of wisdom is fear" (Prov. 1:7). The Old Testament is not talking about psychological fear but ontological fear, radical amazement, humility. Perhaps the best word is *awe*. Awe, wonder, holy fear is the first step toward God and the basis of all philosophy, all religion, all prayer. Skip that first, long step and prayer becomes a mockery. We are reduced to monkey business, as we repeat the words, rituals, and techniques of the mystics without sharing their awesome interior dispositions, their incommunicable experience of the ineffable Godhead.

That is why Jesus never taught prayer and obviously never intended to, until his disciples begged him. Then he taught them the Our Father. He taught them this very short prayer—much shorter in Aramaic—and went off to pray alone. Apart from liturgical prayer there is no evidence in the New Testament that Jesus ever "shared" his prayer by praying with anyone. Prayer erupted from him in the midst of others, but he never pushed it; he was never preoccupied with it. That makes sense. Really deep prayer is always spousal and therefore cannot be shared. There is a level of being in everyone of us that can only be exposed to God. Shared prayer is helpful to some people some of the time, but it must not be exaggerated and should never be imposed.

"Taught" prayer is so liable to become arbitrary and artificial that Jesus never wanted to teach it. He did something better, something that would lead inevitably and authentically into prayer. He induced his followers to live—boldly, daringly, creatively. He seduced them into the mystery. He knew that if he could inspire them to live fully, to keep them moving unself-consciously into the heart of the mystery, then he would eventually evoke from them very naturally and spontaneously a prayer of the heart. Remember what St. Anthony of the desert said: "He prays best who doesn't even know he is praying."

Prayer is a cry of the heart; essentially, it is the cry of the Sacred Heart. It is the Spirit in the heart of the historical, mystical, and cosmic Christ, calling *"Abba,"* "Father." Strictly speaking, there is only one prayer in the whole world, and that is the prayer of Christ, the enfleshment of the Word, as he continues to reveal the perfect love of the Father and to uphold the progressively mature response of the Son. We don't always have to come up with a red hot prayer of our own. Prayer is going on full tilt in the lion-lamb of God marching before generations of men and women with a single word on his lips, *"Abba,"* and the eternal canticle of love rising like music from his heart, broken wide open in sacrifice for the sake of the world. All we've got to do is climb aboard and live in Christ.

The specified, meditative periods we usually call prayer are specially designed periods for concentrating on who we are, who God is, and what is going on between us. These daily "concentrates" of prayer do not ordinarily affect us the way vodka does. We don't get a kick out of prayer. Whatever good results accrue to us in the long run from being faithful to prayer, most of us find that specific periods of prayer do not often provide any immediately satisfying experience. But that's all right, since the unsatisfied desire for God is the most important desire of all, involving a joy no pleasure can match.

We have all seen the liturgy ruined by an exaggerated attempt on the part of the "liturgy planners" to achieve some kind of immediate experience of personal warmth and enhanced sensitivity. We would be better off with a dull liturgy than with bad taste. If we are mindful of the enormously complex mystery of the Mass, it can hardly be dull. If the Eucharistic celebration is normal, at least the celebrants and the symbols don't become distractions. The Mass is prayer *par excellence.* The less intrusive, talkative, and fussy we are at Mass, the more prayer itself erupts. We must remember that the Mass is the terrible mystery of our communion in the sacrifice of Christ. Whatever we learn about prayer, we learn from praying the Mass, which is the school of all prayer. Every other type of prayer takes its meaning from the sacrifice of Christ.

Even the darkest and driest forms of prayer make sense because Christ makes sense. It was in Jesus' own darkest hour, in his failure and in his death, that God vindicated him and raised him up. The strength of God was manifested in the weakness of Jesus' passion, the glory of God in the foolishness of his love. The Gospel paradox is: If you do not love, you will have no vitality; if you do love, you will collide with the "empire" of human egotism and become a fatality. Jesus chose to love and to die—with no way out of the dilemma—and so must we. A serious outbreak of love would be more a threat to the world as we know it than the nuclear arms race. Jesus' poor community of love was a threat to the establishment, and so he was killed. But he was raised from the dead, and that is the final message of the Gospel. God made sense of the whole disastrous love affair that started in Galilee and culminated on Calvary. It was the greatest victory of all: the triumph of failure.

At the end Jesus did not tie up loose ends and secure the Kingdom. He simply loved us faithfully and the Kingdom came from the Father as gift. In a talk given at Blackfriars in Oxford, Herbert McCabe, O.P., got to the root meaning of gift and the radical meaning of prayer. He is worth quoting at length:

> A gift means an expression of love. When we thank someone for a gift we are thinking through the gift to the giver. ("Thank" and "think" come from the same root.) To say thank you for a gift (or as the Greeks would say, to make a eucharist of it) is to recognize it, to think it, as a communication of love. Gift is an expression of

an exchange of love. To believe in the resurrection, to believe in God, is to believe that the resolution of the tragedy of the human condition comes as gift, as an act of love encompassing mankind. The crucifixion-resurrection is the archetypal exchange of prayer and answer to prayer. On the cross Jesus casts himself upon God, not because he has not come of age, not because he lived before the age of technology and therefore lacked the means for constructing the kingdom, not because he needed a "god in the gaps" to do what science and sociology might have done had he lived two thousand years later, but because he was wholly human, wholly free, wholly loving, and *therefore* helpless to achieve what he sought. If he had wanted something less than the kingdom, if he had been a lesser man, a man not obsessed by love, he might have settled for less and achieved it by his own personality, intelligence, and skill. But he wanted that all should be as possessed by love as he was; he wanted that they should be divine, and this could only come as gift. Crucifixion and resurrection, the prayer of Christ and the response of the Father are the archetype and source of all our prayer. It is this we share in sacramentally in the Eucharist; it is this we share in in all our prayer. But the crucifixion, the total self-abandonment of Jesus to the Father is not just a prayer that Jesus offered, a thing he happened to do. What the Church came to realize is that it was the revelation of *who* Jesus is. When Jesus is "lifted up"— and for John this means the whole loving exchange of the lifting up on the cross and the lifting up which is the resurrection—when Jesus is lifted up, he appears for what he is. It is revealed that the deepest reality of Jesus is simply to be *of* the Father.

Jesus' prayer is not incidental or sporadic. It is what makes him who he is. Jesus is not a genius at prayer. He is sheer prayer. In other words, his place in the Trinitarian love-life, his personal, altruistic relationship to the Father, is revealed as fully as possible (as much as we can bear) in his passion, death, and resurrection. The prayer of Jesus that is his crucifixion is the matrix of the web of exchange in which we are all involved to the extent that we are really alive and truly in love. For us to pray is for us to be taken over, possessed by the Holy Spirit, which is the life of love between Father and Son. To pray we must become Love's prey. That way our prayer will never be artificial or contrived. It will always be a cry of the heart, ultimately the cry of the Sacred Heart. That is the kind of prayer that Jesus promised would always be answered.

True prayer depends essentially on the initiative of the Father drawing us into the Son. It is God who prays. We become the locus. But God does not act in a vacuum. He needs our bodily locus. He does not act compulsively; nor does he intervene from outside. Divinization is always an inside job. The Word was made flesh. God suffuses all being. Though I do not exhaust his Being, he is my innermost self. If I do not impede him, he will Christen me and transform me into the contemporary Christ.

Becoming the locus of God does not happen automatically or easily. It requires an unflagging discipline of life issuing in personal, passionate presence. Mary is the supreme example of this basic human disposition. Out of the enormous psychobabble produced by our psychological, schizoid society, there is one meaningful cliché that can be applied unequivocally to Mary of Nazareth: she really had it together. She was *all there:* not obtrusively, obstreperously, or pretentiously—but self-effacingly.

In other words, what locus requires of us is focus. And here I must say something specific about prayer in the city. If you really live, you will pray. Life in the city is not natural enough. This is true of the average person in the city; and it is true in all levels of existence: play, work and sex. None of these dimensions of city life is natural enough or human enough and so seldom leads to prayer.

City life has become so dehumanized that a person may be

born into any one of our proliferating megalopolitan mon-
strosities and go through the whole number of his years on
earth without ever once becoming conscious of the simple
beauty of a tree on the pavement catching the lamplight, or
the rain falling. It is no wonder that the elements, harnessed
now to satisfy nothing less ignoble than man's grossest material needs, seem to be on the point of taking their revenge.

We all can't live in the wilderness, though almost everyone
should retreat there periodically. So we must learn to focus
in the city. Here are a few suggestions:

Live each day deliberately. We can trace all sin back to
thoughtlessness: We were caught off guard and ended up off
target. Certain situations (cheating, lying, damaging) *seemed*
to be good because we were not perceptive or insightful
enough; we did not see things as they really are, did not discern the connections. We did not know that the fat lady was
Christ. You cannot love what you do not know. It takes time
and energy to know, to really understand. Above all, it takes
stillness.

Do what you are doing. But really do it. Put all you've got
into it. Live on the spot where you are. Are you sweeping
the floor? Then sweep as if the whole world depended on it.
Are you making love? Then make love as if there were no
tomorrow. Are you playing ball? Then play with all your
might. Are you having a drink with a friend? Then drink and
commune until you are seized by joy. Are you suffering? Then
embrace it gladly and "fill up what is wanting to the passion
of Christ" (Col. 1:24).

*Stop doing half the things you are doing in order to do the other
half contemplatively, that is, with loving awareness.* Action without contemplation is blind. You cannot give what you do not
have. Our problem is dispersion of energy. Our actions must
be far more selective, discriminating, informed. Doing must
be an overflow of being. The most important thing to do is

to be. The only valid form of work, ministry or apostolate is *contemplative* action. Noncontemplative activists are phonies. People in the ministry who are not sent, do more harm than good. God does not send anyone unless he has already touched him and begun to transfigure him. We are not asked to be impeccable snobs, but simply *touched* sinners.

Get up early in the morning. Get a jump on the day. Take charge of your life. Do not let too many things happen to you. Recollect your scattered energies, your fragmented self. In the silence and solitude of early morning be consciously rooted in and refreshed by God, source of all life, and then move into the day creatively glorifying God by every distinctively human word and deed.

Have a good read. Otherwise you will be beaten to death by the majestic trivia of the unreal world. A read a day will keep the devil away! Next to unlived life, poor reading or no reading at all causes most of the problems of prayer. Since you are so busy, skip all the good stuff. Read only what is best, for instance, the Bible, the classics, the lives of Christ and the Saints, or fiction such as *The Brothers Karamazov, The Diary of a Country Priest, The Chronicles of Narnia, Incognito.*

Enjoy as much beauty as you can. Waste time festively with your beloved or your friends. Walk in the desert. Stretch out in the park. Go to a museum and savor the art. Listen to good music. Take a long loving look at a child, an old man, a beautiful girl. Go to church and just bask, adoringly in the glory of God. Play with reckless abandon.

Work as creatively as you can. Inject more and more meaning into life, treating everything reverently. Your whole life is your spiritual life. As John of the Cross taught, "Where there is no love, put love, and you will find love." Then when it comes time to pray—that high time of the day—when God wants to deal directly and immediately with you in an unspeakably wonderful encounter of love, you will be ready. It is the presence of God shining all day long diaphonously through all that is real, and your awakened response to these multiple epiphanies in your busy workaday world that prepares you for this moment of spousal prayer.

CHAPTER 4

Prayer: A Cry of the Heart

The more people hear about prayer, the more convinced they become that they cannot pray. So they give up the bit of praying they have been doing or repress the recognition that they cannot pray. Then they feel forced, privately and publicly, to concoct such a shrill and strident cackle of pious cacophonies that they cannot hear God say: "Be still and see that I am God" (Ps. 45:11). He is saying that to me all the time. And it's never the same. One way or another it startles, staggers, and then steadies me. I love, and learn so much by the way he varies his inflections. His multifarious inflections lead to my myriad reflections. Sometimes he accentuates the "be," sometimes the "be *still*," and at other times the "see." But lately he has been teasing or tormenting me with a whole new emphasis on the "I." "Be still and see that *I* am God." In other words: "let go of your hold, relax, and let me be God."

This is the beginning of prayer and the root of prayer: the recognized fact that we cannot pray. I am telling you nothing new. Long ago St. Paul said it to the Romans (Rom. 8:26). If we begin with this lighthearted (not lightheaded) conviction, most of the obstacles to prayer will be precluded.

We don't need to be pious, religious or spiritual in order to pray. We don't need a keen sense of the presence of God. Since prayer is rooted in our existential situation and in our sensibility, its evocation and growth depend more on our experience of the absence rather than the presence of God. We pray not because we are full but because we are empty; not because we are strong but because we are bereft. Prayer is the cry of the heart in protest. Here I am feeling needy, lonely, God-forsaken; and yet, deep in my inmost soul, I know with a certainty that cannot be shaken that I am created, graced and personally called to be with God, closer to God than a wave to the ocean or a ray to the sun. I am in God the way Christ is in the Father and the Father in him. If only I could "put on the mind of Jesus" (Phil. 2:5) and enjoy Christ-consciousness! But even then my prayer would be a protest. How could it be otherwise when I am so privileged and so outraged, when I know his presence and feel his absence.

Being bonded and branded by God, there is bound to be a sustaining and substantiating kind of impalpable but vital peace, but groovy and gushy—never! Because prayer centers and orders our existence, there will always be a treacle of tranquility to resist the tremendous tedium and the tumultuous tantivy of life in the world. But as long as prayer is inescapably terrene, it can never be *merely* serene. The prayer of the real mystic is earthy, not heavenly. I do not worry about the "poor" and the "little ones" being lost; I worry about their being spoiled by the high-muckamucks of the Meditation Movement and the manufactured "highs" of the Charismatic Movement. Apart from unexpected moments of glee and occasional uncontrollable ecstasies, our prayer, like Jesus' prayer, is apt to be pretty pedestrian. We should not think of prayer as a titillation of the diaphragm or even a sudden exaltation of the spirit, but as a quotidian transformation into Christ. The more I pray, the more I think and love and act like Christ.

What a scandal it is for followers of Christ to aim at grand achievements of meditation and high degrees of prayer! How preposterously petty to complain of emptiness! The Son of

God emptied himself so that we might have eternal life and share the absolute wildness of God in our humble circumstances on earth. "His state was divine, yet he did not cling to his equality with God but emptied himself to assume the condition of a slave, and became as men are; and being as all men are, he was humbler yet, even to accepting death, death on a cross" (Phil. 2:6–9).

On the cross he reached the peak human experience. The apex of his prayer was expressed not in some kind of seraphic jubilation but in terrible ululation, an agonized atheistic howl: "My God, my God, why have you forsaken me?" (Matt. 27:46). Every human being can identify with Christ; everyone can live enough to laugh or cry or suffer. And that is all we need to pray. Whatever evokes a cry of the heart can cause prayer.

It is precisely out of our Godlessness or Godforsakenness, not out of our piety or our religiosity that we pray. This is our offering to God. Long before wisdom comes fear, and long before the ecstatic sigh of intimacy comes the anguished cry of pain. How can we sincerely pray for the coming of the Kingdom, a radical transformation of our lives—not an improvement but a revolution—if we are already fairly satisfied and feel pretty good? How can we be bowled over by the beauty of God if we enjoy kitsch and schmaltz? No wonder we do not howl or bellow! We live so securely and superficially that all we can come up with is a chirp or a whimper.

Anyone who is at all in touch with reality will be fundamentally dissatisfied with the way things are, with the brokenness of our world and our lives, with the rape of the earth, with the absence of God and the delay of his Kingdom (his coming) for the sake of a demonic empire that thrives on our immediate gratification and our ultimate degradation.

God has promised himself. The world is dying for him. The world needs bread, but "Man cannot live by bread alone" (Matt. 4:4). The world needs God infinitely more. We can arrange lavish liturgies, but is it prayer? We can measure astonishing degrees of altered states of consciousness, but is it prayer? We can muster millions into an evangelistic fever, but is it prayer? We can groove on Jesus, edify one another by our God-talk and even impress ourselves by our highly polished pietistic orisons, but is it prayer? He alone prays who has the moral audacity to move awesomely and unstintingly further and further into the promise of God, where, finally, any human contrivance is out of place, and only a divine mode of being is appropriate. At this point the prayerful person becomes more mystical and more earthy than ever. Disarmed, stripped, utterly vulnerable, such a person is ready to be divinized: not only ravished by God contemplatively, but used by God actively in the military-industrial complex as well as in the political, socio-sexual wastelands. No other kind of person, regardless of power, prestige or genius, provides any hope for the world.

Only God can address God. That is why we must "pray unceasingly" (Eph. 6:18) until the Spirit fills us and we are transformed from being pawns of the empire into being sons of God, and our petty petitions become the prayer of Christ. Our incapacity for prayer is not a temporary impediment; it is a permanent part of our condition. The Spirit prays in us when we live enough and want God enough. It is not enough to be ninety percent alive. We must be one hundred percent alive. It is not enough to want to want God. We must want God. And we must want him unequivocally and without reservation. We all know this, but we repress it because we are all torn apart by an illusory loss. We fear "lest having God we have naught else besides." We temporize and barter until death comes, losing our souls in the meantime—the "mean" times because there are no high times. But Christ said: "Trade till I come" (Luke 19:13), and he desires with infinite desire to come *now*. And he would come now if we would trade everything, be dispossessed and surrendered—his, utterly.

As St. Augustine said, wanting God is what prayer is all about. When you want God, you don't want you. When you want you, you want Christ at a safe distance. You want his peace without his sword. You want his illuminating flames but not his consuming fire. You want a small god to whom you can talk casually and before whom you can sing and dance and saunter away unsundered. When you can do this repeatedly without shame, then know that your religious quest is a sham. When you want God, you want Christ to come with his sword and rip you to shreds.

I almost rephrased that last blunt sentence for the sake of decency and balance by introducing the concept of ego as distinct from self. Then it occurred to me that you might do what I do: wage war against the peripheral ego and pamper the primordial self. It is a subtle temptation; and when capitulated to, it leads inevitably to a lifestyle that is sophisticated and respectable enough, but behind the thin facade, it is hopelessly ramshackle, or, as my young neighbor Kevin Ward would say, tacky.

This absolute response to the Absolute, this personal, passionate presentation of oneself to the devastating demands of Love *is* prayer. Whether private or public, it is common. It is the longing and the striving of the communion of saints. It is the positive, noble plight of the mystical body of Christ. It involves the history of humankind and the evolution of the planet.

This writing was just interrupted by the prayer of pathos. Hunting season just opened in Nova Scotia. The woods all around our hermitage are full of hunters—not hungry, priestly men who need to feed their families and hold at bay the wrath of God by animal oblations—just rapacious sportsmen driven to kill, for fun and trophies, the innocent, beautiful, helpless creatures God has given us to take reverent, loving care of, while they, by their wild *life*, keep us young of heart. While the violent explosion of gun powder rents the air, what can I do but pray? God suffers in the wounded deer, the dying stag, and the pathological sports-hunter. I must identify with them all in the prayer of pathos. (Either that or hunt the hunters!)

A poem entitled "Hi" by Walter De LaMare comes to mind:

> Hi handsome hunting man
> Fire your little gun.
> Bang! Now the animal
> Is dead and dumb and done.
> Nevermore to peep again, leap again,
> Eat or sleep or drink again. Oh, what fun!

Such sarcasm exposes the macho-muddle and the idiotic flapdoodle that tries to turn the primitive hunt into a modern sport. This painful interruption accentuates the point I am trying to make about prayer. It is what all the people do together to gather the whole planet into more life, into universal harmony, into Christ-consciousness, into realized union with God.

INTERCESSORY PRAYER

Intercession is one of the basic forms of prayer. It is based on the teaching and example of Christ, the fellowship of the whole human race, and the solidarity of all created beings. It hinges on our interpersonal relationships and our coresponsibility for the common good of man, the well-being of one another, the evolution of the earth and the purposes of God in the world; that is, the revolution of Christianity. We pray for God to come to us, to be with us, or rather to reveal and manifest his passionate presence already there but hidden. We pray for *his* Kingdom to be established and our proud and powerful empire (imp-power) to be vanquished. We long for a new heaven and a new earth.

Prayer, however, must take actual and concrete form. It is in the exposed particularity of our needs and neediness that God comes to us. Benefactors help young, struggling artists by exposing them to the public and defraying the costs. By intercession we expose one another to God and lovingly bear the burden. We leap into the breach. We forego a safe but stifling insularity for a unifying and deegotizing solidarity that opens us up to the totality of being and, with every prayer, releases the divine, healing love at the heart of things. By intercession we give voice, in general and in particular, to the cry of the world for God, and prepare a worldly way for divine disclosure and human fulfillment. In this case, I must risk everything. I must see my neighbor in the light of God's promise and in the light of his need. I must seek the neighbor's dire need—what he really wants, not what I halfheartedly wish. And if nothing seems to happen, shall we attempt to comfort our friend with mealymouthed words of embarrassment and convenience? Or will we bellow with him in the wilderness, protesting the absence of God and the helplessness of man? I think Dylan Thomas was right when he wrote: "Do not go gentle into that dark night, but rage, rage against the dying of the light." Everyone, like Jesus himself, longs for company in Gethsemane. That company should be rousing, not resigned.

Here I think the West, in conjunction with the Christian Orthodox tradition of the East, should be making a highly significant contribution to the religious development of the world. Saints of the Eastern Orthodox tradition, along with the American Indians, have taught me more about prayer as a cry of the heart, and particularly intercessory prayer, than have all of the seers of the Hindu-Buddhist tradition. I am sure that what I have to say now about the prayer of intercession is due in large measure to what I have learned over the years from Metropolitan Anthony Bloom.

As the great Catholic Archbishop points out, there are some

marvelous images in Scripture that indicate very graphically the meaning of intercession. For instance, in the Book of Daniel, King Nebuchadnezzar condemns three men, binds them up in chains, and tosses them into a fierce and fiery furnace. Coming subsequently to look on the ordeal, to his utter astonishment and amazement, he sees four men walking freely in the flames. He addresses himself to his counselors and his ministers and says, "Did I not bind up three men and throw them so bound into the fire to be tortured and burnt, and do I not now see four men walking freely in the flames and does not one of them look like the son of the gods?" (Dan. 3:92). That is a good image of the God we pray to. Christ, God Incarnate, Christ, the most beautiful, attractive embodiment of God, is the supreme intercessor. The whole meaning and purpose of the Church is to be the prolongation of the presence and power of Christ in the world of today and tomorrow. Intercession is the very essence of the Church and of the Christian life.

Two other scenes depict this in the New Testament. One is portrayed by Mark, who describes Christ walking on the waters (Mark 6:45–52). His disciples are in a panic because they are caught in a squall, in a tempestuous storm, and death is about to snatch them away. There is nothing between them and death except a few flimsy planks. They are distraught; desperate, crying out for help. In the distance, walking calmly away from them, they see someone who looks like Christ. But how could it be? How could this be Christ in the midst of the storm, walking on the waters, in the waves, facing the turbulence, caught up in the terror and the horror of the storm? Is not Christ supposed to be the center of peace, tranquility, serenity, order and harmony? So the disciples think it is a ghost, a monstrous apparition. But it is, in fact, Christ. And that is where we always find him; not on the seashore, not on the edge of the lake inviting us into a calm snug harbor. We find him at the eye of the storm, at that terrible still point where all the violence of the world collides and is dissolved in his presence.

Matthew depicts a similar scene where the apostles are caught again in a terrible storm and are again hysterical (Matt. 8:23–27). Death is about to devour them. Waves are lashing at the boat and filling it with water. They are about to die. Christ lies asleep in the bow of the boat with his head resting on a pillow. The apostles don't cry out in prayer, a prayer built on faith, but they cry out in anger, out of faithless anguish: "Are you going to let us die?" They could easily have added, "If you cannot save us, then at least share our last agony with us!"

This is the attitude of millions of men and women in the world today in regard to prayer, God, and Christ. We think of God as a distant God who may indeed hear our prayer and sympathize, but who is not there in the midst of the storm, who is not in the horror, not in the terror, not in the flames, not in the death, not in all the human hells possible in this world. But that is especially where he is. He is the suffering God.[1]

Remember Job? We very often think of Job's patience in terms of his ability to bear all kinds of affliction and torment, but his real patience lies in his waiting for God. There was no answer to all his probing questions, representing all the vexing, poignant questions of mankind, except Christ. He summed up all his questions, his pain, his agony, in this question: "Where is the man who will come and stand between me and my judge, put his hand on his shoulder and mine, and bridge the gap, heal the breach? Where is such a man?" (Job 9:33). That was his prophetic plea for Christ. And that is what intercession is.

Intercession is the act of the incarnate God. We must cling to that act tenaciously. We think about intercession in paltry terms. We either remind God or exhort him to do something that he has neglected. We remind him what was said in *The*

New York Times about death in Rhodesia or war in the Middle East, and our prayer becomes more of an affront to God, who is infinitely more aware of what goes on than any of us, or all of us, could ever be. Intercession does not denote, first and foremost, a prayer. It denotes an action.

SALTATORY PRAYER

Intercession is saltatory and not hortatory. Saltatory means leaping. Hortatory means exhorting. Intercession consists primarily of leaping into the breach and being there, just as God was in the fierce and fiery furnace, just as Christ was walking on the water and lying in the boat. Intercession must be saltatory first of all: an incarnational, existential action. Grafted on to that act is the possibility of prayer. But there is no possibility of hortatory prayer without first being saltatory, leaping into the breach. Intercession, therefore, begins with an involvement that is definitive, total, complete, unconditional. The interceding Christ is not primarily, essentially, a praying Christ. He is secondarily a praying Christ. Primarily, essentially, he is the God-man, in action, *pro nobis*, in act for us. He is the son of God who became man, the Word of God who became flesh, and in him the breach was healed, harmony was restored. In the perfect humility and obedience of Christ, man and God are united forever. The cosmic conflict, the whole conflict of the universe, the conflict of disordered, chaotic man, is focused and concentrated in this man who is the Pontiff, the Mediator, the New Man, and in him the whole conflict is brought to an end.

A key word governs every dimension and aspect of prayer, especially intercession, and gives us an insight into the deepest meaning of intercession, and that word is *solidarity*. The solidarity of Christ, and therefore we who are called to follow Christ and to be Christ in the contemporary world, is our own solidarity, and it is twofold: a solidarity with God and a solidarity with man. It is the suffering of God and all his divine disclosures (*pati divina*), and it is the suffering of man and all of his foibles, his failings, and his possibilities (*pati humana*).

How far does this solidarity extend? We understand when we reflect on the Gospel event of Jesus plunging baptismally into the Jordan (Matt. 3:14). There is a tremendous difference between the baptism of those who surrounded St. John the Baptist and were baptized by him, and the baptism of Jesus. All the others plunged into the Jordan first of all to be washed, to be cleansed, and secondly, to be washed and cleansed interiorly, to be rid of the "stinking lump of sin" that separated them from God, that made them so miserable, so inhuman. It was a matter of penitence. They repented and were made new.

Jesus, who identified himself with man and every aspect and dimension of man, including the burden of sin (without being sinful), plunged into the same murky waters that carried the terrifying sinfulness of mankind in its tides. He did not plunge in out of penitence, but out of passion. That was the beginning of his passion: the passion to be totally at one, not only with God his Father but with man, particularly man in his pain and suffering.

It is remarkable that we have so much in common with Christ; everything except sin. We share even death, and yet it is here where we are most different from him. Christ is by nature immortal and therefore cannot die. That is why I think the greatest miracle of all is the death of Christ—a greater miracle than his resurrection. How can he, who is immortal by nature, who is God, possibly die? Because he became so identified with man, embraced manhood, so clothed himself in manhood even in human death, that he suffered the burden of man; therefore he suffered the absence of God, the loss of God by which men die. He died and was rejected by man because of his solidarity with God, and he was abandoned by God because of his solidarity with man.

Intercession begins with involvement. It is continued in fidelity and completed at the cost of our own life. As we know from the Apostles' Creed, Christ even descended into hell. Sheol, the hell of the Old Testament, is infinitely worse than any hell depicted by Dante. The hell of the Old Testament was that one place where God would not be and never could be: it was the total absence of God. Christ entered into death, passed through death and descended into hell. This abominable, hateful, impossible place became full of the translucent brilliance and the incandescent glory of God himself, so that hell, the Sheol of the Old Testament, came to an end and no longer exists.

The fact of Incarnation, of absolute solidarity, is the act of intercession upon which is grafted Christ's prayer, a prayer which is true precisely because it is undergirded by the act. It is no verbal acclamation, "Lord, Lord" (Matt. 7:21). It is rather an accomplished, unforgettable fact. And so, today and forever, Christ the supreme intercessor stands before God his Father in heaven with his brilliant wounds of battle shining in his hands, his side, and his feet. That is the unquenchable fire, the unforgettable accomplished fact that is intercession. All pure, true intercessory prayer is grafted on that act of the redeeming, self-sacrificing, humble, obedient, faithful Christ. Our prayer is true, pure prayer insofar as it is grafted on to that same body of Christ, full of the same meaning and the same validity.

Our vocation is to be what Christ was. It was very difficult for the apostles to understand what this supreme, supernal vocation implied. Remember how shortly after Jesus described, with some eloquent detail, his own passion and death, James and John asked him if they could sit at his right hand in the Kingdom (Mark 10:37). Why did they ask that? Because at the end, as a summation of his whole passion, death and resurrection, Christ said, "In three days the Son of Man will arise" (Matt. 20:19). The apostles forgot all about the passion, the cross, and the death as prerequisites, and zeroed in on the reward. They became preoccupied and inordinately attached to the possibility of glory without the cross, of resurrection without death, of conviviality in heaven without fellowship on earth, of an eternal destiny without sharing the earthly exile of Christ, their head. On Good Friday Christ was murdered on a cross, and on the following Sunday he said to his followers, "As the Father sent me, I send you" (John 20:21). The image is clear: sheep being sent into the midst of wolves to live and to be slaughtered, to be sacrificed and reborn: the whole process leading to the new man, the resurrected man, the triumphant Christ. There is no other way.

All intercession hinges on this. No one can be foreign or external to the mystery of Christ; no one in the Old Testament, and no one in the New Testament. Christ suffered the loss of God more radically than any other man in the history of the world. Any other form of atheism is a drop in the bucket, a drop in the ocean, compared to the loss of God, the radical absence of God that Christ experienced. Why? Because of his solidarity with man, with the whole of mankind and every ounce of man's suffering. When we partake of the Eucharist, we are actually committing ourselves to the cross. We are longing ardently for bliss, beatitude, perfect freedom, for the beatific vision, for endless heavenly life— but through commitment to the cross. They are inseparable.

NOTES

1. I have discussed "the suffering God" at greater length in *Mystical Passion* (New York: Paulist Press, 1977), pp. 25–32.

CHAPTER 5

Birth of the Outlaw Church

We have banalized the desert experience, robbed it of its intrinsic, dynamic worth, and made it a shibboleth. We must make every effort to rescue the "desert experience" from the trivializing process set in motion by the cognitive minority (theological camaraderies, spiritual experts, rocking chair philosophers), the prayer-conscious pietists, retreat addicts, disjointed or disillusioned individualists, and losers in general who like to dignify their self-afflicted plight with a holy and now respectable designation—a "desert experience."

It would help to locate the desert experience in the Judaeo-Christian tradition and then indicate the purpose and shape of such an experience in and for the world today.

ABRAHAM

The Bible story really begins with Abraham, the father of those who believe, who penetrate more deeply into all of reality, who become suprarational, that is, *more not less* reasonable, by actually living by faith.[1] Those who journey into the wilderness with this nomad do not simply subscribe to a set of beliefs, nor do they merely make sporadic acts of faith. The whole of their lives is rooted in a faith experience. They see what God sees, love what he loves, and do what he wants. They belong to him. They have been apprehended by God.

To be lovingly seized by God is a terrible good. A twofold response is inevitable: sheer terror at being exposed to his holy scrutiny and his implacable will; exquisite delight in belonging to him. But before anyone can belong to God, he must be wrenched away from his idolatries.

Until he was apprehended by God, Scripture seems to tell us, Abraham had shared in the idolatrous beliefs of his people: "In times past your fathers, down to Thare, father of Abraham and Hahor, dwelt beyond the River (Ur was in Mesopotamia) and served other gods" (Josue 24:2, cf. Judith 5:8).

Abraham was called to leave Chaldea, situated in the "fertile crescent" around the north of the Syrian desert, the cultural and religious capital of the known world of his age. At God's command he had to separate himself from the "establishment," to go he knew not where, to find he knew not what. He did not know when or whether or how he would again have a home or a land of his own. And yet as he rose to follow the inscrutable call of the wilds, God promised that through him the nations of the world would be blessed. "The Lord said to Abraham: 'Leave your country, your kinsfolk and your father's house, for the land which I shall show you. I will bless you and make your name great. . . . In you shall all nations of the earth be blessed' " (Gen. 12:1–3). In response Abraham promised his God that he would lead a different kind of life: a life different from the cultured and the religious peoples, whether urban or nomadic, among whom he was to make his pilgrim way.

God commanded Abraham to start something absolutely new, which implied a break with all that had been before in the religious sphere. When Abraham journeyed by faith into the wilderness, he inaugurated the revealed monotheism, which has remained the common treasure of three great spiritual families who recognize him to be their ancestor: Jews, Moslems, and Christians.

To achieve this brand new goal, to earn his divinely promised inheritance, Abraham had to become an outsider, indeed, an outlaw—not selfishly and destructively, but self-
lessly and creatively—for the glory of God and the honor of
his people. His disestablishment—his desert experience—is
the original revolution: the creation of a distinct community
with its own deviant set of values and its coherent way of
incarnating them. Today it might be called an underground
movement, a political party, an infiltration team, or a cell
movement. The sociologists call it an intentional community.
Then they were called "Hebrews," a title which probably
originally meant, "The people who crossed over." That is
why "passover" lies right at the heart of the whole biblical
drama. It is also our most urgent need today if we are to
break out of our self-imposed prisons of everydayness, our
sybaritic institutions, our business as usual, our petty pie-
tisms, and political paltriness.

St. Paul spoke of the salvation of the nations in terms of
the mystery that has been hidden from eternity in God, who
created all things, and restored all things in Christ. But the
whole *historical* process of incarnation and reconciliation began with Abraham. That is his unique grandeur. On the
threshold of sacred history, he was the first to whom God
told the secret of his plans, to whom he entrusted the knowledge of his mysterious ways. That is why Irenaeus calls him
the first of the prophets. For prophecy is the understanding
of the mystery of sacred history given by the Holy Spirit,
who alone fathoms the depths of God.

The mystery of history is the divine pleasure God finds in
sharing this Trinitarian love-life with man on earth. Who can
fathom that secret? But it is that secret and its promise, made
originally to Abraham and climaxed in Jesus, that keeps us
going and prevents the world from falling apart. That is why
Walker Percy, an outstanding contemporary Catholic novel-

ist, says that children of Abraham should live with a vivacious and contagious enthusiasm, as though they were obviously "on to something."

Abraham was on to it. So was his wife, Sarah. They beheld the *mirabilia Dei*, the reality of history unfolded before them, as they clung blindly and without sensible support or social security to the "promise." For that *is* the promise—the manifestation of an irrevocable design, when faith leans, unsupported by trumped-up experiences, on a reality firmer than anything perceived by sense, because it is actually based on fidelity to God. Through Abraham God entered into history and made man his cohort. Abraham faltered before God's incomprehensible presence, as under a weight too heavy, heavier than flesh could bear. Scripture tells us that he was seized by a kind of ecstacy or loss of his senses, "a great darkness."

That is the desert experience—darkness: all the lights go out, fashions fizzle, idols topple, structures crumble, attachments are sundered, ordinary supports are withdrawn. There is nothing but a veiled God and a promise—what we now call the Hebrew Covenant. Abraham staked everything on that promise. And on this nomad's fidelity to that promise, God staked the future of the world.

> The salvation of nations is still an object of faith and expectation, as it was for Abraham. But just as Christ's raising people from the dead prefigured the final resurrection of the Last Day—and, as K. L. Schmidt remarks with such depth, the very fact that those who had been raised died again shows that their raising was merely a figure—so for one unique moment in history, on the day of Pentecost, the Holy Spirit united all the nations represented in Jerusalem in one common language and thus fulfilled in figure, and, as it were, in seed, the promise to Abraham, which will be made at the end of time.[2]

Abraham turned his back on the overdeveloped civilization of Chaldea, moved into the desert where he lived in tents tentatively, that is, "on the move"—not compulsively or convulsively as we do today, trying to squeeze God in, taking his name in vain, either piously or profanely, as we attempt to catch a train or bus or plane or beat the traffic on the highway. No, Abraham moved deliberately. He moved alone at the same pace as his browsing sheep, his ruminating camels and his fat wives. He freed himself of baggage and bondage and lived in utter simplicity, enjoying a rhythmical relationship with all aspects of his environment. It was in this eremitical, nonviolent milieu that this semitic nomad, this outlaw apprehended by God, started the original revolution. The revolution thrives on faith. Faith is nurtured by prayer. Prayer is a cry of the heart. Praying is not going into a church, but into a promise and relying on it.

MOSES

Abraham received the promise and lived by faith. Moses heard God's name and saw his glory. Abraham moved from the bright shiny surface of things to the obscure inner suchness of things, from the city to the desert, and learned to cope creatively with the real world by living deliberately in the realm of pure faith. Abraham crossed over. He initiated the passover. Moses, another outlaw (he killed an Egyptian and fled to the desert), was enthralled by God in the wilderness. He taught the people the *way*. ("Way" is a better translation for the word *Torah* than "law.") He taught them the way out of illusion and fantasy into reality and truth, out of mediocrity into totality or wholeness, out of Egyptian thralldom into eremitical freedom, out of a comfortable slavery into a challenging liberty, out of small pleasures under tyranny into ecstasy under the boundless mercy of the One True God.

Moses was the perfect desertman, the model contemplative: though ravished by God, he was consumed by social concern. And though it was a perilous adventure, at the command of God Moses went back into Egypt to beseech the Pharoah "to let my people go" (Exod. 5:1). Moses was neither a mighty god nor a mere symbol, so he returned to Egypt reluctantly. Elie Wiesel, who is closer to Moses than to his next-door neighbor, insists that Moses' reluctance was due not to fear of the Egyptians but to his disgust with the Jews. What disgusted him? Their addiction to slavery, their obeisance to the Pharoah, their attachment to "the way things are." Their refusal to risk their lives for the sake of their vocation, their election by God. This is what frightened Moses: the immobility and stolidity of his own people, who remained unmoved by God, who lured and wedded them through their father Abraham. This stiffnecked race would never know the thrill of divine allurement nor the Olympian joy of spiritual marriage without the desert experience. So Moses, the greatest leader of the Old Testament, went back into the maelstrom of Egypt, awakened the Jews from their slumber, shook them out of their dumbfounded torpor and led them jubilantly through the Red Sea into the desert. And there in the desert God fashioned himself a new people—strong, united, indomitable—and readied them for the fulfillment of the promises he made to Abraham.

God was faithful. But the Jews faltered. They did not keep the promises their father Abraham had made; nor did they follow unfailingly the way Moses taught. Pure faith is not reached by many for very long. Most of the pressures of most social structures are against it. The Jews were surrounded by life styles diametrically opposed to pure faith. And so God raised up one prophet after another whose clarion call was always the same: return to the desert. Through the desert experience of the Old Testament, God educated the Jews and prepared mankind, bit by bit, by one gift after another for the coming of Christ.

The Old Testament flowed into the New Testament, the city and the desert met, the gap was bridged, opposites were reconciled in the desertman, the wildman, the outlaw *par excellence*, John the Baptist. His was the voice crying in the wilderness: "Make straight the way of the Lord" (Matt. 3:3). He lived for the one joy of hearing the voice of the Beloved. He heard it. He pointed out to his followers the lion-lamb of God. He baptized him. Then he departed, decreased and was beheaded for the sake of the Kingdom Christ came to proclaim.

MARY

The Blessed Virgin had a most crucial role in the first coming of Christ. In her culminated all the expectation of the Jewish people. She was the epitome and incarnation of the long waiting of twenty centuries. The training period was over. The indispensable disposition of mankind—wise passiveness, openness, receptivity—was achieved in the God-centered personality of the Virgin Mary. God would come as an infant once mankind had built a cradle. Mary was the cradle. She was the marvelous flower sprung out of the desert, out of Israel.

Sometimes water seeps through a crack and after many years fills an enormous space; at other times, due to some terrific pressure, there is a deluge of water gushing up and flowing over instantaneously. So it is in the Old Testament: most of the time, awareness of the mystery of God is gradual, if not sporadic. Then suddenly, through some individual or event, an inexhaustible density, an inexhaustible mass of faith is revealed. Thus at the end of the Old Testament, Mary, the woman wrapped in silence, emerges with incomparable force. Hundreds and thousands of years of stammering quest are concentrated and burst forth in this valiant Virgin's *fiat*.

Read and meditate on the "Magnificat" (Luke 1:46–55). In the whole body of Jewish and Christian literature, few texts are more widely known and more vainly repeated than this song of the maiden Mary. What it says is the language, not of sweet maidens, but of Maccabees: it speaks of dethroning the mighty and exalting the lowly, of filling the hungry and sending the rich away empty. Mary's praise to God is a revolutionary battle cry.

How droll and wonderful that the revolution should be brought to a head by a young Jewish girl whose singular role was to bear Jesus into the world and then let him become even more fully and unbearably the Christ!

The word *revolution* has, in the past few decades, become so trivialized that much of its meaning has worn off. But the fact that a word can be prostituted or violated does not erase its real meaning from our serious agenda. The old word, the technical term, for the change Mary was rejoicing in is *Gospel*. But *Gospel* has become a tired old word too. For us today revolution does seem to be the best translation of the root meaning of the term *evangelion*. Literally, it means good news—not just any welcome piece of information, but news which impinges upon the fate of the community. The good news of the New Testament, of Jesus' message, is of such magnitude that once heard in earnest, it will turn your head around. And that is precisely what the Gospel is all about: *metanoia*, repentance, a radical change of mind and heart. In Jesus' time, therefore, as well as in ours, revolution is the point: the judgment of God upon the present order and the imminent promise of another one. That is the point the Gospel makes. And the purpose of Christ is to get to the point.

CHRIST

The only way Jesus could get to the point was as an outsider—the greatest outlaw of them all—a title earned not by destroying the law but by fulfilling it. There was never a desertman like Jesus—not Moses, Elijah, or even the Baptist himself. Compared to Christ the others almost seem like dandies. Is this a preposterous form of hyperbole, an outlandish exaggeration? Not at all. Jesus' outlawish behavior was prompted by the urge toward the achievement of renewal. The Kingdom that he proclaimed was in this world but not of it. The Kingdom he represented was fixed on totally different values, standards, and alternatives. There was no place for him in the establishment. He did not fit. He had to cope creatively with the impossible situation. The opposing force that would wipe him out was not bad men but a pretty poison that seeped unnoticeably into the finest institutions and the most upright men of his day. Jesus was caught in an inescapable collision between the awful justice of God and the entrenched and hallowed powers of the day. The creative quality of Jesus' outsider behavior brings clearly to light the remarkable difference between Jesus' criminality and that of the typical gangster. The gangster's behavior is merely reactionary, whereas in Jesus' case the objective is to change the world. The positive nature of Jesus' rebellion is made clear in the innovative achievement of both his life and his message: "Behold I make all things new" (Rev. 21:5).

Quoting Isaiah, Luke says that Jesus was "reckoned with transgressors" (Luke 22:37). The Greek version uses a more specific word, *anomos*, which means outlaw. Irrefutable historical data prove that Christ was an outlaw.

The first historical fact: there was in Jesus an irrevocable tendency to spread downwards toward the poor and the lame, the outcasts and the sinners. Many biblical scholars maintain that the stable at Bethlehem and the shepherds in the field are mere myths. But Ernst Bloch's observation is provocative, if not compelling: "People pray to a child born in a stable. And the stable can be taken as true for no one would have dreamed up so humble an origin for the founder. Legend constructs no pictures of misery and certainly none that endures a whole lifetime. The stable, the carpenter's son, the fanatic among deprived people, the gallows at the end, such data come from history, not the air." [3]

Once Jesus comes out of hiding, there is no doubt of his position. He is a partisan. He stands with the oppressed. He sows the seed of unrest among the lower classes, always seeking a positive effect: a combination of radical dissatisfaction with an absence of envy. Jesus' nonviolent attacks against rigidity and authoritarianism made him a true stumbling block to all forms of authority—parental, bureaucratic, educational, economic, and military, including the philosophical and theological ideologies that accompany and support them. He not only appealed to the lower classes, he identified with them: "Foxes have holes, and the birds of the air have nests; but the Son of man has nowhere to lay his head" (Matt. 8:20).

Even though he came out of the desert and was not engaged in mortal combat with the powers and principalities of the cities, Jesus' desert experience continued. It is what undergirds and empowers, as well as authenticates, every bold move he makes in the city. Christ's downward tendency reached the pits when he chided the leaders of the people with immoderate acerbity: "The tax collectors and the harlots go into the Kingdom of God before you" (Matt. 21:31). According to Matthew, this was said to the chief priests and elders.

We can see here the emergence of "a rebellious expansion of human consciousness" that is opposed to long-embedded attitudes of servility. In proposing his own ideas, Jesus had not cast out the devil with the power of Beelzebub, that is, by grabbing power himself, brandishing swords, and plun-

dering palaces. His method was to announce the imminent
end of all power structures and chains of command, for which,
instead, he holds a special place reserved—in hell.[4]

The second historical fact that clearly situates Jesus as an
outsider is his extraordinary independence of family. How
often he made a point of this. Without family ties he had no
class. He was nobody. But still his society had to reckon with
him. As Bloch put it, "He who died on the cross was a rebel
against convention and established power; he was one who
raised questions and dissolved family bonds."[5]

The third historical fact is so indisputable that it alone
clearly identifies Christ as an outlaw. Jesus was arrested as
an enemy of the law and murdered by the Romans as an
enemy of the emperor. The crucifixion of Christ, executed
by law outside the city, indicates plainly that the delinquent
had placed himself outside the accepted order of things. Out-
laws were executed outside the gate.

We reach the apex, the high point of the desert experience,
with Jesus hanging on the gibbet. The wilderness prepared
him for this foolish finality. And it was done with disgraceful
dispatch—outside the gate, outside in the horror and darkness, in the Place of the Skull on Dead Man's Hill.

He hangs there still, in agony until the end of the world—
the great Outsider, the holy Outlaw, while we cuddle up inside, safe and sound within the protective walls of normal,
everyday life, within the walls of routine, secular sanity,
within the mendacious molds of our social institutions where,
as Dostoyevsky's Grand Inquisitor said, we are forced to lie,
and where Christ with his disruptive freedom cannot come
again.

He hangs there still—outside the gate, while we become
ever more glamorously and innocuously religious. Where can
I find the pure, still center, free from infection, worry, inse-
curity? Where can I find the still center where the dizzy wheel
no more revolves? Where heaven can be kept safe above and

hell chained secure beneath? Where I can be ordinary, comfortable, born again, saved, baptized in the spirit, one of the faceless masses, anonymous, unchallenged?

Our quest is not religious at all. It is not spiritual. It is a popular psychic phenomenon. It is an ego trip. All we want is boundless bliss, cosmic consciousness, an oceanic feeling, a merger (not union) with being. What a shocking revelation the crucified Christ is: the center—dead center—is outside.

Jerusalem is a magnificent city, a sacred city, reeking of religion. But Jerusalem is off center, reeling to destruction. The city is condemned. Why? It chose convenient holiness inside, while it tried to nail the enfleshed wildness of God to a tree outside the gate.

THE CHURCH

The rulers soon discovered that they could not entomb God's wildness by killing and burying God's Wild One. The brand new peoplehood, the new society Christ created to embody and perpetuate his irrepressible and unrestricted spirit of love, continued to proclaim and to build the Kingdom of God. This society called "The Church" had to contend with the world that killed Christ and re-present Christ to that hapless world. The Church instituted by Christ was an outlaw Church. And only to the extent that it remained an outsider could it, like its founder, be effective in the world and speak with authority.

When we speak of Incarnation, it must not mean God sanctifying our society and our vocations as they are, but rather his reaching into human reality to say what we must do and what we must leave behind. The freedom of the children of God is not the freedom to do whatever we want to do, but what we must do to become holy with the holiness of God, that is, to become fully human and completely alive. Not all of life is to be blessed; not all human efforts can be penetrated by the glow of divine indwelling. The Incarnation is a discriminating and selective enfleshment of the Logos. God's pattern of Incarnation is that of Abraham, not Constantine.

The Church is neither the chaplain of the state nor the soul of society. She is more like a gnat on the rump of society. She is certainly a minority and cannot oblige the world to be Christian. The Church should never have attempted to Christianize the world by controlling it. She must pluck away on the outside and never luck out on the inside. The outlaw Church is the only community whose social hope is that we need not rule because Christ is Lord. It is precisely her position as outsider that dispenses the Church—enjoins her—from pushing people around. The Church cannot afford a respectable inside position. She must begin her work in the wilderness and finish it outside the gate. Her whole ministry depends upon her fidelity to the heart and soul of the Judaeo-Christian tradition: the desert experience. What changed between the third and fifth centuries was not the teaching of Jesus but the loss of awareness on the part of the Church of both her eremitical nature and her minority status. Instead, she fancied herself establishment.

THE LIVELINESS OF THE CHURCH

The vitality of the Church is unmistakable whenever she acts out of her eremitical depth and in virtue of her outsider position. In every such instance it becomes obvious that she has crossed over. And her passover is the source of her unrestricted and contagious love, her exquisitely human relationships.

The following are some outstanding signs of her aliveness.[6]

Martyrdom—Events or movements that alter the life of the Church, either by raising her consciousness or by intensifying her love, have a power that proceeds outward from a radical center and ultimately affects ordinary Christian people. In the early ages of Christianity, a few martyrs at the radical center changed the whole Church. Martyrdom, of course, is one of the simplest and most direct ways of following Christ, and one of the most trenchant ways of speaking to the world.

But it is easier to die for Christ than to live for him. All the followers of Jesus must be so anxious to live for him that they are willing to die for him. Without this kind of ultimate commitment, we are already dead, despite a flurry of activity and a good bit of noise. One way or another, the only life-style fit for the Christian is heroism. At what price discipleship? As T. S. Eliot wrote, "not less than everything."

Monasticism—After Constantine the Church took up a prestigious position inside the establishment. The acceptance of Christianity by the empire made being a Christian easier than ever, and the comfort of that vapid peace between Church and empire was dulling the faith all over the world. Being a Christian was no challenge at all: in fact, it magnified most, if not all, the worldly possibilities, such as political power, material possessions, etc.

The vast majority of Christians did not follow the Fathers into the desert, and yet their exodus changed the whole Church profoundly. The monastic movement that grew out of their flight to the desert nourished the faith of Europe for centuries. It presented a challenge and a high ideal that raised the level of belief, religious practice, and morality for all Christians. The Fathers' creative subversion, their simple and radical renunciation, cut powerfully through all the subtleties of religion and reminded ordinary people that behind all the argumentation was the simple Gospel challenge: "If anyone wants to be a follower of mine, let him renounce himself and take up his cross and follow me" (Matt. 16:24).

A much more radical reformation of monastic life is required of us today if we are going to rescue society from its narcissistic waist-high culture. It is not enough to tidy up monasticism. It must be totally transformed and revivified. Only then will it be a vital force in the Church and a vibrant influence at the creative center of our culture. As in all previous ages, Christian renewal depends upon monastic renewal.

Missionary movement—The missionaries, combining the virtues of the martyrs and the monks, enlivened the Church. Sacrificing ordinary comforts and conveniences and risking their own lives, they spread the Gospel. They, too, renounced all things in order to follow Christ. The missionary movement reminded people back home in Christian Europe that most of the world was not Christian.

But today the missionary movement is more urgent than that. The Church needs to strip down to her bare essential Christ-self and become very deliberately and freely a missionary people, with nothing to say to the world but the Gospel truth, nothing to show but her wounds, nothing to give but herself.

Mysticism—Wherever the Church lives vigorously, mystics abound. Whenever the Church minds her own business, mysticism prevails. Wherever the Christian Church fails to share her most precious heritage, there is a mass exodus to the Orient. If the vitality of the Church could be measured by numbers, the paramount question would be: how many mystics are there?

The mystic is one who is consciously immersed in the mystery, the mystery at the heart of the universe: the passover, the crucifixion-resurrection. This mystery of love has gone on in creation from the beginning. It reached its exquisite climax in Christ—most manifest in him when he hung as a helpless outlaw on a gallows outside the gate. There is no greater love than this. The Christian mystic is the contemporary Christ. He transfigures all the scabrously raw matter of the world by his fierce and universal love.

These are some of the signs of the living Church and her

significance to the world. If this significance is to be renewed today, the Church must renounce any pretension to a
control mode of relating to the world and exercise fully her
contemplative mode of existence. She will do this most surely
if she will "return to the desert" and be the outlaw Church.

"I will espouse you, lead you into the desert, and there I
will speak to your heart" (Osee 2:14).

NOTES

1. Pascal's famous conversion was a conversion "to the God of Abraham, Isaac and
   Jacob, not the God of the Philosophers and scholars." To Kierkegaard and to
   Chesterton, "The perfect thinker was Abraham, the father of faith, and not Soc-
   rates." To Abraham, faith was a new dimension of thought, which the world did
   not yet know, which had no place in ordinary knowledge and simply broke through
   the restraining truths of our experience and our reason. As Jean Hering notes:
   "The model for a Christian is not the princess in exile who longs to return; it is
   Abraham setting out toward an unknown country to be shown him by God." Cf.
   Jean Danielou, *The Advent of Salvation* (New York: Paulist Press, 1962), p. 29.
   If contemporary Neo-Catholic Pentecostals shared this patristic insight into the
   meaning of prophecy and Pentecost, the Pentecostal Movement would move in a
   direction opposite to its present course.
2. Cf. Jean Danielou, *op. cit.*, pp. 32–33.
3. Ernst Bloch, *Das Prinzip Hoffnung* (Frankfurt, 1959), p. 1482.
4. Adolph Hall, *Jesus in Bad Company* (New York: Holt, Rinehart & Winston,
   1972), p. 111.
5. Bloch, *op. cit.*, p. 1490.
6. A. Placa and B. Riordan, *Desert Silence* (Locust Valley, New York: Living Flame
   Press).

CHAPTER 6

The Call: Personal, Particular, Persistent

I love the link between the Old and New Testaments. I love our Jewish heritage. If I'd had my own choice, I would have chosen to be a Jew. I love that rich and robust tradition out of which we were born and nurtured. Many people think I'm a Jew, even a rabbi. I was driving through Boston one day and a group of hitchhikers said, "Hey, Rabbi, give us a lift." I did. I am not a Jew. But there is a lot of Jew in me because I am a Christian. There is no way to become a full-fledged Christian unless you first become a good pagan and then a good Jew. Then perhaps you can become Christian—by the grace of God and one miracle after another and one human gigantic effort after another.

Isaiah, one of the greatest of all Jews, said: "I heard a voice saying, 'Whom will I send? Who will go for us?' And lo I answered, 'Here I am, send me' " (Isa. 6:8). That is the divine call to all of us, a call that is personal, particular, and persistent.

The call is extremely personal. In the very beginning, God personally approaches, encounters, invades the privacy of Adam and says, "Oh, Adam, where art thou?" (Gen. 3:10) That is the universal religious question of Hinduism, Judaism, Christianity: "Oh, Man, where art thou?" The only answer is existential presence. If we were to answer verbally, we might say haltingly and fearfully: "Here I am, Lord, standing defenselessly and transparently in your presence. Take me, possess me, seize me, consume me, and then if you will, if it is your good pleasure, send me into the world with your message, your scorching words and your flaming love."

Throughout the Old Testament God's call is equally personal. God approaches Abraham, not as a force, not as an abstraction, not as an idea, but as a super-personality. He invites Abraham to leave his home and his land and move adventurously, unknowingly into foreign territory to become the father of our faith: Jewish and Christian. How I love the *Jewish Connection!* It links us up with the living God. Not ideas about God, or ambassadors from God, or messengers from God, but God himself. God approaches Jacob, not in an aloof, distant, comfortable sort of way. He encounters him and involves him in intimacy, in a wrestling match. We must all learn to wrestle with God and come out of that terrifyingly wonderful encounter as Jacob did—maimed for life; not with a nice experience of a surrogate God, but transfixed, transformed, remade, reborn. Jacob came out renamed Israel. And throughout the whole rest of the Old Testament God remains in hot pursuit of Israel, who is his bride. There is no love affair like it in the history of the world until it culminates in that mysterious love affair with God embodied in Christ.

The whole personal theme is accentuated more than ever in Jesus who became the Christ. Jesus always speaks to us personally. "Will you personally follow me?" (Matt. 4:20) "I am the bread that you must eat" (John 6:51). In that Eucharistic crisis his pseudo-followers left him. He turned to his intimate followers, his faithful ones, and said, poignantly, pleadingly, "Will you too walk away from me?" (John 6:7) Later on, to the same intimate followers he said, "Are you ready to drink the cup that I must drink?" (Mark 10:38) "Will you not watch one hour with me?" (Matt. 26:41) And then finally, hanging from the cross, he shouts down through the corridors of the centuries into every hidden canyon of the world, "I thirst" (John 19:28). With that cry he expresses the thirst of man. It is up to each of us—terrifying, impossible vocation!—it is up to us to represent and to satisfy both thirsts: the thirst of man for God and the thirst of God for man.

All the old philosophical and all the new scientific theories that try to cope with the ineffable God in terms of an abstract life force are ridiculous failures, including an extremely popular, contemporary version: the fatuous inanity of *Star Wars*. God is not a life force; God is the extremely mysterious super-personality that invades the whole world, the whole earth, the whole universe, and the heart of every human being, every animal, every vegetable, and every creature—*personally*. He is involved. A famous theologian who died a few years ago, a very holy rabbi, Dr. Abraham Heschel, developed a whole theology of pathos emphasizing the fact that God is not a separate God. He is infinitely distinct and utterly transcendent but not separate. God is more me than I am. God is closer to you than you are to yourselves. God is in history. God is in the world. In fact, of him alone is it possible to say unequivocally, "He is."

The second quality that characterizes God's divine call to us is this: *The call is particular*. Here we have the celebrated scandal of particularity. You may recall that distinguished British writer, Hilaire Belloc, and his peculiar refrain: "How odd of God to choose the Jews." Odd indeed! If we put all our rational strengths together and were as reasonable and logical as mankind can be, we would conclude that God should have chosen the Irish! But he didn't: he chose the Jews. Not only did he choose them, he clung to them, he invaded them, and he persisted and remained faithful to them. He will unto the end. Even today the Jewish community is so cohesive and so implacable that it cannot be dissolved and cannot be destroyed. The Jews have been, and are, and always will be the chosen people. Particularity. Not any race, not any people, but the Jews. Of them, from them, Christ came.

God does not act in a vacuum or pull full, live, integrated human beings, holy men, holy women, saints, out of hats. He acts incarnationally through all the marvelous, messy dimensions of our fleshy, dirty, wonderful world. God chooses a particular person. And God through Christ establishes a particular institution: the *ecclesia*, the Church. He endows it with powers and delegates it functions that in no way can belong to anyone or anything else. Other groupings may be celestial, ethereal, esoteric, euphoric, but they do not perform the solemn, official prayer of the Church. They may engage in corybantic and sanctimonious forms of bacchanalia with pepsi-cola but these are not sacred liturgy, the Eucharist, or the sacramental representation of the ineffable God embodied in his most attractive form, the terrible, wonderful living Christ. If the Communists ever went on a genuine anti-Catholic rampage and wanted to destroy the Church, they could do it—if we would tell them the secret. They would simply have to destroy all the bread, the wine, and all the priests, and they would wipe out the Church. That's how earthy the Church is. That's how incarnational she is. And that's how particular God is.

Thirdly, God's divine call to us is passionately *persistent*. Think of how God chose Moses, a wanted man hiding in the desert. God sought him out and sent him back into Egypt to free and liberate the Jews who had become respectable, comfortable slaves. God does not want slaves. He chose one towering man to go back into Egypt, where he was wanted for having killed a man, and free his people. God is always that persistent. After Moses came a succession of prophets whom God chose, invaded, and imbued with power from on high. They were so overwhelmed that one after another—Isaiah, Jeremiah, and Elijah—all said: "Enough! Leave me alone!"

But God would not leave them alone. God is never finished with us. If we think he is finished then *we* are finished. God never finished with Israel. (It is highly significant, therefore, that the prime minister of Israel today should have a name that cannot be interpreted as finished!)

At the end of the great succession of Jewish prophets came a little girl who summed it all up. God always does this in his peculiar, reckless, lavish, creative, ingenious way with little people. A Jewish girl recapitulated it all in herself. She stood before God and his high proposals of love and said, "*Fiat*, yes, take me, let me be your self-effacing, self-oblivious instrument. Let Christ come." He came through Mary and through her valiant, virginal *fiat*.

Then came Christ himself, the man who was born priest, not delegated by the people to be one. He was and is essentially priest. He exhausted his priesthood. Today there is only one way to respond to the call and that is to climb into the heart of Christ. There's only one way to get wet; get into the water. Only one way to enjoy the powers of being Christian and that is to be thrust by the Church into the heart of Christ and to share his own Sacred Heart.

Christ was not only priest; he did not only perform ceremonies; he was also the victim. He not only offered sacrifice; he was the sacrifice himself. Thus he is the exemplar of all priesthood. We, too, must not only celebrate immolation; we must be immolated. We must not only offer sacrifice and oblation; we must be the sacrifice and the oblation. It is a terrible thing to be called by God. We are marked men and women. But bold and brave and daring enough to bear the divine burden, to be the suffering servant, and to die. Out of our death, our positive, dynamic victimhood, our suffering life, comes rebirth and resurrection and therefore delight and joy.

God's devastating demands require a response. There is only one way to respond to the absolute, and that is absolutely. Our response must be as personal, particular, and persistent as the divine call. Once we experience that *personal*, I-thou encounter and say yes to God, God will brook no whiny nay-saying. On the day that we back off from God and refuse to say yes, despite devastation, the lives of all of us are imperilled. Our responsibility is that personal. We actually cushion God. We cushion his blow: both his love and his anger. For if God is the infinite lover, he is also the dreadful God of wrath. The measure of his anger is justice; his motive is compassion for the victims of human cruelty.

If we spent the rest of our lives in the woods or in the desert unseen and unheard, our silence and our solitude would be justified by this alone. There are ten other good reasons that cannot be mentioned here. But this reason alone: staying the angry arm of God, is reason enough for some people to remain hidden in a life of joyful penance and prayer. In Deuteronomy 9:19, Moses says; "I was afraid of the anger and the hot displeasure which the Lord bore against you so that he was ready to destroy you, but the Lord hearkened to me." That is our prophetic vocation.

The second quality that must also characterize our response to God's personal initiative and divine call is *particularity*. We must stop referring to the abstract God and awesomely say from the depths of our hearts, "*My* God." This "myness" is born out of personal, intimate experience. We have been touched. We are and always will be sinners, but we are *touched sinners*.

I was paddling one of our canoes on the Nova Nada lake. A wind came up, and a heavy current. I had a difficult time paddling home. Even though my arm was beginning to fall off, I found that if I stopped, I would be blown back half a mile. So I had to keep going. That is the kind of passionate *persistence* that must characterize our daily, ongoing, unending response to the divine initiative. It's extremely difficult. All the pressures of our society militate against it. But despite all the shallow, superficial qualities of life, despite the mediocrity and the compromise that is acceptable and respectable, a man or a woman can be free enough to say yes to God and belong to him and so become Goddened, Christened, and united with Him.

Prosaic functionalism keeps us from fulfilling our prophetic, poetic vocation because we are overly impressed and victimized by our roles. If vocation meant more to us than position, success, and excellence, then perhaps doctors would be more willing to make night calls, nurses would be more willing to be available on holidays, and there would be very few mechanized answering services and recorded messages. Everything would be far more personal and therefore far more devastating, but divinizing.

What does prosaic functionalism mean? It means making it with the world, with the flesh, and with the ego, instead of making it with God. If you are going to make it with God and bring to fruition this love affair initiated by him, then you have got to die to the world, to the flesh, and to the ego. That prophet of old, Elijah, addressed all his enemies and said, "Why do you go on limping between two Gods? Choose one or the other. If your Lord be God then serve him; if Baal be God then serve him, but stop limping back and forth. Stop compromising. Take a stand and be" (I Kings 18:21). When Alexander Solzhenitsyn addressed graduating students at Harvard University, he said that the Western world is in decay. The reason for this decline, this failure to come to the rescue of the impoverished, destitute world, is that the Western world has lost its roots in its Judaeo-Christian tradition. It's that simple.

CHAPTER 7

Lost Christianity

Since the inception of the modern age, there has been a steady decline in religion, while people everywhere manage to remain half-heartedly engaged in the enervating pursuit of mundane values. But the socio-political activity, the high-tech ventures, the military-industrial concentration and the sexual permissiveness have left everyone notoriously dissatisfied. It is hard to imagine a more disgruntled and dyspeptic society than the crowd of bored blokes we refer to as "modern man." We tried alcohol, drugs, and sex to no avail. They only worsened our condition. Then we diluted our religion and distorted a very promising psychology initiated by Freud into a damaging psychologism—a pseudoreligious psychidolatry—which took two forms. One form lifted us above the dreadful tedium of daily life and out of the reality of life and death encounters into a facile facsimile of life by enabling us to achieve a placid accommodation to the social conventions of the crowd, and to accept, however mediocre and mendacious, the lowest common denominator of the resounding and respectable majority. This type of psychologism won for us a vapid peace.

This first psychidolatrous twist characterizes most of the services and therapies provided by the churches and the psychologies. These services and therapies help us to survive as part of the "crowd" and to get on "nicely" in the world. The measures taken to serve and to heal amount to a system of compromises that leads to a respectable form of mediocrity; and the whole palliating, patchwork process is based on a lie: the assumption that we can, in a merely human way, with appropriate religious and psychological techniques, cure a soul.

The government renders the same fallacious services when it uses merely political techniques to mend a city. Such civilized mendacity sucks the unwary into the secularized and sophisticated commonwealth of spiritually impoverished people. At the same time it teases them out of the divinized commonweal, the earthy mysticism of the body of Christ.

How opposed to the teaching of Jesus, who assured his followers that only his Father, by the power of the Spirit, could cure and make them holy. Jesus himself said he was the Way to the Father (cf. John 6:66). He did not provide any help for our getting on in the world; he enabled us to get to God. He did not offer a program of accommodation to the values of the world but a blackmail of transcendence: *now* what does God require of me? He offered freedom in the life and death revelation of the whole truth about man. He promised that the meaning of his own passion and death, once it grasps and ignites us, will make us free. Ignited truth is existential. Once we become fire, we are embarked on our own passion and death, and therefore the Christian revolution of love, and consequently, the resurrection.

The truth about man is staggering because the mystery of man is unfathomable. It is therefore a mistake for the contemporary Vatican II Church to try and adjust to the social-cultural milieu of our day. Church teaching must be deeper than that. It must come to terms with and convey to us in as lively and limpid a language as possible the age-old truth, the perennial philosophy, the heart of the Gospel, pure and undefiled. The undiluted Gospel message has nothing to do with living successfully according to the standards of the world. The Gospel, grasped and lived, ushers in the Kingdom; or, more correctly, when we actually follow Christ, reenacting his passion and death in our own way, we build up the Kingdom already established by Jesus. There is a subtle but salient difference between his "Kingdom" and our "empire." His Kingdom is based on Christ-realization, our empire on ego-fulfillment. The therapists underestimate humans by adjusting them to the "mean" rather than alluring them to the pinnacle of all human aspirations. The ministers of religion overestimate the people by preaching the unitive way while skipping the purgative and illuminative steps.

The essential Christian message is *metanoia*. *Metanoia* requires a radical change of mind and heart. This axial shift, this rediscovery of our own truly personal center, is not an effort of will to improve some superficial aspect of the psyche or to overcome some fault or vice. It is, above all, a courageous trust in life. More specifically, it is an unconditional confidence in the Christ who was handed over to death, descended into hell and suffered separation for us, for me.

We need a redeemer, we need a savior, because we cannot sanctify ourselves. No matter how cold-bloodedly dutiful or perseveringly prayerful, we cannot save ourselves. Our graced nature is to be engaged in an unmapped exploration into God, to be in passionate pursuit of an Other. And the Other saves us. To the extent that we are self-made like the Pharisees or remain neutral like Pilate, we let the prostitutes and the publicans go first into the Kingdom. These poor creatures enter before us because they know they cannot save themselves, because their pitiful condition opens them to divine love. The root of sin is our pretension to save ourselves, our obsession with grades of righteousness and marks of goodness provided by the law, our attachment to security, which moral superiority brings. Will we ever understand this scandalous teaching of Jesus? Probably not till the end. That is undoubtedly why Dostoyevsky says in *Crime and Punishment:*

> Then (at the Last Judgment) Christ will say to us,
> "Come, you also! Come, drunkards! Come, weaklings!

Come, children of shame!" And he will say to us, "Vile
beings, you are in the image of the beast and you bear
his mark, but come all the same, you as well!" And the
wise and the prudent will say, "Lord, why do you welcome them?" And he will say, "If I welcome them, you
wise men, if I welcome them, you prudent men, it is
because not one of them has ever been judged worthy."
And he will stretch out his arms, and we will fall at his
feet, and we will cry out, sobbing and then we will understand all, we will understand all! Lord, your Kingdom come! [1]

Have the psychological and ecclesiastical institutions even
begun to tap the *infinite* aspects of the mystery of man, the
abyss of woman? This deep dimension is attested to much
more authentically by the blood of the martyrs, the mindfulness of the monks, the fidelity of intrepid warriors of God
bonded together forever in friendship or matrimonial love.
These are the disciplined wild ones who scrap conformity to
the world for the sake of transformation into Christ. Although the levelling egalitarianism and the dehumanizing
pressures of conventional society are against them, these genuine Christians have tremendous support in the dogmatic
foundation of the Christian view of man: Trinitarian theology.

The Trinity doesn't have a social or community life. The
Trinity is social, community life. No one of the Persons of
the Trinity is or has any kind of being in or by his or her
own self. Each one is eternally constituted in being by a total
devotion and absolute donation to the Other.

We are the image and likeness of God. Who can fathom
us? Who can get a handle on us? How can we be pigeonholed
or stereotyped? How can anyone condemn us? How can we
consider ourselves depraved? How can any real self-knowl-
edge be safe, shallow, or soporific? Who can say—without
fear and trembling—"I'm okay, you're okay"?

If we are made in the image of the incomprehensible God,
then we must share to some extent in that incomprehensibil-

ity. If there is an apophatic theology, then there must be an apophatic anthropology. If God is hidden, so is man. True knowledge of the human person is unknowing, and so theological anthropology must never be an attempt to reduce the irreducible nature of man. If we are to really know one another, in our mutual unknowing, then we must face the high degree of risk and respect that will be demanded of us. Once God created man in his own image, he in some way limited himself, and once man fell and went his own way autonomously, God only truly came to know man again on the cross. At the heart of unknowing that leads to true knowledge—the direct awareness of the heart—is infinite vulnerability.

Knowing oneself and a few significant others takes a lifetime of focused energy, of active and passive recollection. It is easier to know the heavens than ourselves. That's why there are a lot more nature lovers than saints. We will never come to know ourselves unless we achieve a balanced, dynamic rhythm of solitude and community. This vital rhythm itself needs to be inspired and sustained by our attachment to the living, mystical tradition of the Church. The Church Fathers' God-centered humanism, their Trinitarian emphasis on the mystery of man is obviously and delightfully not an item in an academic syllabus but of life-giving importance for a world in which ideologies conspire to reduce man to one-dimensional fatuity. To the degree that psychology and religion have identified with the paltriness of our national culture or the trendiness of modern man, they have failed to do much more than comfort us and cheer us on in our Gadarene rush to the sea.

THE DANGER OF DOWNWARD
SELF-TRANSCENDENCE

The other form of psychologism plunged us below the frivoling antics of stuffy or giddy human beings on the soporific surface of life into the dark and demonic subsurface levels of existence, where, though we suffered terror and disintegration, we felt generally alive and individually unique.

The roots of our lives lie in other worlds; that is why our deep-seated urge toward self-transcendence is so implacable. If we are not set free by the way of the cross, if, because of our abhorrence of suffering and distaste for discipline, we part from Christ and cease to participate creatively in his passion and death, if we fail to grow in the loving awareness of God, fail in some way to anticipate the Resurrection—then we will be forced into some bogus liberation either below or to one side of our genuine personality.

That is why alcohol and drugs are devoured so voraciously by men and women all over the world. Always and everywhere human beings have felt the radical inadequacy of their personal existence, the misery of being their insulated selves. More than anything else, they all want the awareness, if only for an hour or two, if only for a few minutes, of being someone, or, more frequently, something other than the insulated self. "I live, yet not I, but something generated by wine, pot or music liveth in me." Even though the self-transcendence is accompanied by nausea, convulsions, hallucinations and coma, the drug-induced experience is considered utterly worthwhile by a worldwide variety and plethora of people. What they experience, of course, is not liberation but enslavement. The self-transcendence is invariably downward into the less than human, the lower than personal.

Like intoxication, elementary sexuality, disengaged from love, is used to extend and inflate the self and so to escape, however briefly, an unbearable insularity. This illusory escapade is sometimes innocent, sometimes squalid.

Despite the enormous popularity of drunkenness, drug addiction and debauchery, civilized people do develop safeguards against such unhealthy forms of downward self-transcendence. But there are no such safeguards and moral outcries against the most dangerous form of subhuman transcendence—crowd delirium. Mob scenes are every bit as dehumanizing as excessive drinking and sexual savagery. But we not only tolerate them. We depend on them. They erupt in the nicest places. I witnessed one recently—a decision-making meeting in a monastery. Deprived of reason and free will, the crowd is reduced to infrapersonal and antisocial irresponsibility. How many of us are inspired and intoxicated by our pilgrimages, tours, political rallies, corybantic revivals, patriotic parades, evangelical crusades and charismatic conventions? The question is: are these meetings really and truly *ours?* Do we really *meet?* Or do we merely react and emote? Far from outlawing this horrible kind of subhuman behavior evoked by herd-poison, the Church and State often capitalize on it to consolidate their own religious and political powers.

In *The Devils of Loudun,* Aldous Huxley describes trenchantly the enormity of this problem:

> In the course of the last forty years the techniques for exploiting man's urge toward this most dangerous form of downward self-transcendence have reached a pitch of perfection unmatched in all of history. To begin with, there are more people to the square mile than ever before, and the means of transporting vast herds of them from considerable distances, and of concentrating them in a single building or arena, are much more efficient than in the past. Meanwhile, new and previously undreamed-of devices for exciting mobs have been invented. There is the radio, which has enormously extended the range of the demagogue's raucous yelling. There is the loudspeaker, amplifying and indefinitely reduplicating the heady music of class-hated and militant nationalism. There is the camera (of which it was once naively said that "it cannot lie") and its offspring, the movies and television; these three have made the objectification of tendentious phantasy absurdly easy. And finally there is that greatest of our social inven-

tions, free, compulsory education. Everyone now knows how to read and everyone consequently is at the mercy of the propagandists, governmental or commercial, who own the pulp factories, the linotype machines and the rotary presses. Assemble a mob of men and women previously conditioned by a daily reading of newspapers; treat them to amplified band music, bright lights, and the oratory of a demagogue who (as demagogues always are) is simultaneously the exploiter and the victim of herd-intoxication, and in next to no time you can reduce them to a state of almost mindless subhumanity. Never before have so few been in a position to make fools, maniacs or criminals of so many.[2]

Many kinds of music have the same intoxicating effect on us as an aroused crowd does. Seduced by the haunting or mounting rhythm, we tend to lose our critical faculties and our poise.

Is the downward movement I have referred to here ever a valid and ethically viable way toward spiritual self-transcendence? My own conviction is that it happens rarely, and even then, accidentally or coincidentally. It is certainly not commendable; in most cases it is very damaging. I do know of a few favorable incidents where stimulants were ingested, physiological changes occurred, and an ordinarily opaque personality became momentarily transparent enough to know what it feels like to be supernaturally alive. In similar circumstances a person may become so sensitized and soulful that he is able to be in touch with the ground of his being, and from that panoptic watershed of two worlds he may, indeed, intuit the Underground—the Holy One, the Wholly Other. But some sort of authentic life of the Spirit would have had to prepare him for this spiritual experience. At any rate, no drug can cause mysticism. It can only bring about physiological changes that may turn out to be, if one is both lucky and blessed, a more conducive psychophysical disposition for a possible mystical experience. Since, even at its best, this is a Peeping Tom mysticism, despite a flashing glimpse of Otherness, its permanent effects are almost always negative, so negative that a state of degradation usually ensues.

Both psychotherapeutic trends of our day—up into a vapid peace and down into vital turmoil—turned out to be nugatory, making either dandies or demons of us all. We dallied with psychological uppers and downers until we couldn't stand it anymore. And then we returned to religion halfway—that is, superficially and superstitiously. That is where we are now, and it seems to be the worst state of all. "A little religion is a dangerous thing." And that's what we've got—a *little* religion—a separate little thing made up of bits and pieces of pious clichés, trendy slogans, and disguised idolatries. We add them like a preservative to the big things that really rule our lives such as the White House, the Pentagon, the Corporations, and the media. But the little thing, with no great effect, seems to coat everything either charismatically or fantasmagorically, especially psychology. The shrinks are beginning to sound like gurus, and the gurus are beginning to sound like shrinks.

Amidst the narcissistic meditations, the paltry or pompous prayers, the dire or dreary do-duggery, and the whole fantastic ferrago of therapeutic religiosity, there is here and there a sure thrust toward the pure heart of religion, and thus, consequently, toward the possible transformation of society and the renewal of life on this planet. One such thrust is Jacob Needleman's *Lost Christianity* (New York: Doubleday, 1980).

When we were kids we prayed: "St. Anthony, St. Anthony, please come around; something is lost and cannot be found." It was a pious tradition that St. Anthony had a knack for finding lost things, so we prayed to him a lot, since we were always losing stuff. Christianity has lost something essential: its abillity to provide an authentic mystical experience, its divinely human capacity to produce saints. Obviously God raises up saints despite the general inadequacy of the churches, but the world rightly deplores and laments the hapless and inept role of the Church in the world with regard to the sanctifying of human beings and the hallowing of the planet.

In the face of this crisis we need to do more than pray about it, and we need more than St. Anthony. With intellectual-scientific acuity and moral audacity, we need to continue the process Jacob Needleman has begun. We need to discover precisely what Christianity has lost and how it can be retrieved. If the decline of Western civilization is to be intercepted, we must relocate and reactivate the very essence of Christianity, what Rudolf Otto's historical-religious classic referred to as *The Idea of the Holy*. Neither Otto nor Needleman uses this "idea" as an explanation of the Holy. These are ideas that are meant to be something other than explanations. Such ideas help us discover the truth for ourselves as opposed to concepts that organize what has already been discovered either by ourselves or by others. These ideas are what the great traditions have called "sacred," and what so many modern authors are fond of calling "esoteric."

Along with the idea of the Holy, Christianity has lost the way to experience and conceive the idea of the Holy so that we are drawn by love even beyond the most sacred idea into personal, passionate Presence, into God. First of all, it must be noted that love has nothing to do with the connubial capers of newlyweds, the unctuous badinage of the "bonded," the evanescent vagaries or visceral aberrations of the swingers, or the spiritual canoodling or firkydoodling of the charismatics. It is in no way related to the morbid mucking about of the moral majority or the ridiculous redundancy of the born-again Christians.

What exactly is required of the lover? Needleman's answer, based on the sacred traditions of the East and his own penetrating understanding of the Judaeo-Christian essence, is: PAID Attention. Note my effort not only to underscore "paid" but to score it through and through the way cashiers do with cash reports and reciepts. There must be no mistake about this attention. It must be paid for—and paid in full! The Gospel challenge is not easy. In following Christ, in tending to "our Father's business" (Luke 2:50), the price we must pay is nothing less than everything. Watching, waiting, searching, and waking up constitute the chief challenge of the New Man, the God-man, Jesus who became the Christ.

INTERMEDIATE CHRISTIANITY

This full payment for attention or loving awareness, or for what the Buddhists call mindfulness—all the inner work and discipline that is required of us even to begin to share the God-centered consciousness of Jesus—this is what has been lost in the West and what Needleman calls *intermediate Christianity*. There are levels of Christianity. We are now in a subnatural (fallen) condition. We cannot enjoy the supernatural gifts until we become natural. We cannot be given a direct experience of God, mystical union, unless we have an experience of our own existence, unless we know what it feels like to be alive. We cannot say "I am a Christian" until we can say "I am." We cannot enjoy the authentic results of religion unless we employ practices that are such appropriate, instrumental means to the end that they do, indeed, awaken the whole personality and activate all the human potentialities. If we go through the motions of religion without putting on the mind of Christ, we engage in monkey business. We copy the external behavior of the holy ones with no idea of the Holy. We might even imitate Christ slavishly without following him creatively into a filial relationship with the Father, into the fullness of life, the perfection of love. The greatest frustrations of all, as well as the most hideous forms of hypocrisy, come from trying or claiming to see God without stillness and purity of heart. In the Old Testament God said: "Be still and see that I am God (Psalm 45:11). In the New Testament God said: "Blessed are the pure of heart for they shall see God" (Matt. 5:8). Intermediate Christianity is learning to be still and achieving purity of heart.

To a very large extent, the fatuous inanities of the contemporary Church are due to the neglect of this existential-ontological level of existence. Unskippable steps are required to attain a perceptive appreciation of ourselves in relation to the Godhead and to behold the manifold in the One. All deeper stages of prayer and richer realms of mystical life depend upon this recollected state of being. No matter what Needleman discusses in his works—religion, philosophy, medicine, culture, education—he unwittingly reaches the same crucial point. In every case the culminating idea is that modern man has forgotten how to cultivate the power of awareness of his own being-in-the-world. So how can he reconcile his capacity for good and evil, his finite and infinite dimensions, his demonic and divine potentialities? How can he integrate and unify all these aspects of his mysterious self into the mystical experience of realized union with God? The lost Christian has forgotten what awareness is. And since you cannot love what you do not know, the lost Christian has almost ceased to love.

Love means what Jesus meant by the word *Kingdom*—the fullest way of being human—a way that digs so doggedly into the heart of things that the digger piles nature upon nature, each more supernatural than the other, until he comes to the abyss of pure spirit; and in that awesome Presence he is overwhelmed. Such a man or woman becomes absolutely still, ravished by the Wholly Other who is recognized in and as oneself but never exhausted by the "self"—not even by the great big Nietzchean, Jungian, or Oriental "Self." Becoming human is becoming more and more actively engaged in the search for the Other. The Other is our treasure. "Where your treasure is," Jesus said, "there is your heart also" (Matt.

6:21). That is why "attention in the heart" is such a central orientation of the Eastern Orthodox tradition of Christianity. And that is why the more natural we are, the more erotic we become, because eros is that primordial passion in us that drives us on relentlessly toward the final love affair. As St. Augustine said, "We cannot rest until we rest in God." The more human we are, the more sexual we become, no matter how celibate, because it is sexuality that equips us for the search, for the treasure hunt. Freud was only half right. What really governs our lives is not the pleasure principle but the treasure principle, though in the end they converge. Humans are most exquisitely human not in sexual congress but in spousal prayer. Prayer is digging in—digging with the heart and the mind down into deeper levels of being until one reaches the Underground, the Infinite and Inexhaustible Fount of our being, the One who said "I am that I am" (Exod. 3:14).

This is the one great "dig" that all human beings—supernatural archaeologists at heart—long for and discover existentially in this totally absorbing and fulfilling treasure hunt. This is "the pearl of great price" (Matt. 13:46) for which we are willing to pay attention. The sacred traditions call this "dig" contemplation: the pure intuition of Truth, born of love. Modern man seems to know that love is the secret, but he doesn't have the secret knowledge, the hidden way, that will open him up to love.

The secret knowledge referred to here has nothing to do with gnosticism, nor with the occult. It was openly disclosed by Christ and richly developed by the early Church. "Many are called, but few are chosen" (Matt. 22:14). Jesus called as many as possible and chose as many as made it possible for him to choose them freely. In other words, between the call and the choice comes the enormously responsible period of intermediate Christianity during which the followers of Christ must, by an unflagging discipline of life, cultivate purity of heart and eradicate in themselves whatever would disperse their energy or divide their attention.

Such a radical transformation of personality is a Promethean program, involving as Needleman says, "the accumulation of the force of inner attention. Stone must become water before it can flow. The pathos of Christendom . . . and of most religions in the modern world, is that of preaching to stones that they must flow into the ocean. In a certain sense, the problem of Christianity is not that something has been hidden, but that not enough has stayed hidden. In other words, in our present psychological condition, we are like stones, and the Christian virtues do not represent what is possible for us until we become water."

Only if we achieve this awakened state symbolized by water can the great ideas and ideals of sacred tradition be rightly received and acted upon. But if in our soporific, subnatural state we get hold of sacred ideas or techniques, we merely incorporate them into our egotistic subjectivity, our waking dreams. Much of what we call religious renewal today is nothing more than propped-up belief systems, new verbal formulas, and old emotions recycled over new objects.

What we need is a new quality of consciousness fired by a new emotion. For this prayerful state of enlightened love we need no new senses and no new nor higher faculties; not if reason is operating at its proper level, intermediately, as the logic of the whole personality. Reason, inflamed and liberated by the vital force of emotion, moves from mere notions into vibrant motions of love. It breaks through all the prisons of rationalism, becomes superrational and ready to be wedded, wounded and utterly transfigured by the Spirit. Enlightening the mind, enlarging the heart, responding creatively to the exigencies of our own being-in-the-world, prepare us for the direct experience of God, for the mystical life. God cannot become man unless *we* become man, that is, authentic human beings, in tune and in touch with whatever is real enough to connect us sacramentally with the source and the end.

LOST EMOTION

Christendom has failed to create a conducive climate for the development of reasonable-emotional persons. It is a curious phenomenon to find such emotional immaturity in a highly civilized society (such as we regard ourselves to be). "Is not *the emotion of a Christian* the 'most lost' element of lost Christianity?" That's how Needleman sums up two long and highly significant conversations he had with Archbishop Anthony Bloom. And then, with a quote from the latter, comes the clincher: "Emotion must be destroyed. . . . We must get rid of emotions . . . in order to reach . . . feeling."

Some clarity could be gained, perhaps, by consistently distinguishing between singular and plural, between emotion and emotions, feeling and feelings. There are unquestionably many emotions, but when they pull together harmoniously they act like a single force, empowering us to move, and move quickly, in one direction. They are like good, spirited, but manageable horses under the deft direction of an experienced charioteer. As a unified force, and in cooperation with the intellect and will, they serve effectually the purposes of the real self (as opposed to the ego); they enrich the quality of meaning, and they intensify the reign of God in our lives. But in a maelstrom of emotions, the mind is fragmented, the heart divided and energy dispersed. Archbishop Bloom urges us to destroy the maelstrom—emotional reactions that are egotistic, automatic and mechanical. In our fallen, bent condition we react thoughtlessly, like automatons. We need to be deautomatized; and to achieve that end we need a rule of life and daily meditative practices. Without meditation and its accom-

panying deautomatization, we never learn *to do just one thing.*
We do not respond deliberately and freely to events, nor do
we choose the situation in which we live. We let automatic
emotions turn us into robots. We are such hollow men that
we do not develop souls. We are such driven men that "the
soul is aborted a thousand times a day."

This attitude toward emotions has a long tradition in the
West as well as the East. A fourth-century monk, Evagrius
Ponticus, one of the greatest spiritual masters of all time,
presented guidelines for the arduous inner struggle to break
free from the sufferings and illusions brought to man by the
emotions and the thoughts that support them. He specified
some of these evil emotions: anger, gluttony, lust, etc. In
fact, he invented the famous list of the seven deadly vices.
According to Evagrius, the capital sins are overcome by
apatheia. By this key term he meant freedom from emotions.
It is the opposite of what we mean by the English equivalent,
apathy: emotional impotence or the incapacity to be. Doing
often takes the place of being—doing things we are forced to
do by our automatic emotions, our inattentive reactions.

St. John of the Cross highlights two emotions that need
special attention: anger and desire. Without these powerful
emotions at our service, we would be lost. The emotion of anger, in its natural function, serves the virtue of courage.
Without courage we wouldn't be able to practice any of the
virtues. And without a puissant assist from anger, we wouldn't
have the courage to oppose evil. We let too many bad things
happen to us, personally and collectively, because we are not
angry enough, because we do not hate evil enough. Love is
not enough to build the Kingdom of God, to foster, cultivate
and increase the common good in this world. We need hate
and anger.

In Psalm 4 we read, "Be angry and do not sin." The RSV
translation turns this inspired word upside down and makes
nonsense of it: "Be angry but sin not." Our old friend Eva-

grius interprets this psalm correctly when he says: "Get worked up against sin, direct your anger against temptations, and so resist sin." Why, as our Lord promised, will the gates of hell not prevail against the Church? Because the embattled Church will be storming hell, just as her Lord did, and not the other way around.

When not defused by self-pity, anger can fire us up with the fire Christ came to ignite (Luke 12:49). Then as fierce and fiery champions of God's rights, we will hardly even notice who has offended or who has neglected us. Consumed with zeal for God's glory, we will forget ourselves. Busy about our Father's business, we would never think of setting up a poky little business of our own. Instead, we wage battle with the enemies of God: sin, death and deceit.

Desire, like anger, is for our own good. Disparate desires disengage us from the one thing that gives meaning to our lives. Purity of heart is to will one thing—the one thing necessary (Luke 11:42). Contradictory desires tear us apart. They cannot coexist. As long as our desires are in conflict, we are in trouble. There will be no peace, no serenity, and no effective action—that is, really contemplative and truly apostolic action. A breakdown of body and a depression of spirit are inevitable. The contradictory desires must be eliminated; the disparate desires reconciled.

This is an important distinction. The possibility of a balanced spiritual life is based on a practiced understanding of this important distinction. If we eliminate the disparate desires instead of reconciling them, we become dispassionate and therefore unchristian.

We must feel our way from the crib to the grave. We must experience one breakthrough after another. I am not referring to peak human experiences. They are too sporadic, and sometimes merely sensational rather than supernatural. I am referring to the experience of God in the day-by-day demands of an ordinary life passionately lived. After all, mysticism is the presence of God felt. But, mind you, it is possible—most probable, in fact—to enjoy wondrously this deep down feeling without being feverishly "excited" or cunningly "esoteric."

What God requires of us is to be lovers of him and his whole world. Can we achieve this without the agony and ecstasy that has branded every lover everywhere during the long history of this planet? How utterly detached we must be from automatic emotions, good feelings, contrived experiences, extraordinary phenomena and the merely decorative trappings of the spiritual life! But just as we know what it feels like to be burnt by the sun and washed by the water, when all of our senses are refined, our faculties activated, our masks dropped, then we will know what it feels like to be touched by God. Despite the tedium and drudgery that seem to dominate our lives, below the majestic trivia of everydayness, we do remember being touched by God. We feel loved and love the feeling—and desire more.

While foolishly flaunted by a notoriously noisy and noxious minority today, feeling is ignored or unduly denigrated by the rest of us. It is confused with sentimentality and regarded as vapid, sweet froth, a temperamental indulgence unbecoming to a serious person. This is regrettable because it hampers the power of love and stifles the human spirit. Emotion is a worthy and indispensable part of the human response, whereas automatic emotions, as we have already noted, control inhuman reactions. We must never forget the continental difference between human response and inhuman reaction. Emotion operates in each case. When we react, we are impelled toward *incoherence*, acting compulsively and convulsively by force of scattered emotional impulses. When we respond, we are led into *coinherence*, which is the really hot stuff of the universe, the Trinitarian, self-sacrificing love-life at the heart of all reality, holding all things together. If we want to know what coinherence looks like, how it uplifts the whole

social, political and ecological world by contagious infection
and how it actuates both evolution (the essential charism of
the West) and identity (the essential charism of the East),
then we must take a long, loving look at Christ.

As the Gospel says, he came to give life, more life than
this world has ever known, infinite life (John 10:10). He
came—this God-man—to give himself. We cannot receive this
life or reciprocate without emotion. Emotion is a vital force
that the will needs if it is to catch fire and not remain only
"the will to love," but actually become love. There is nothing
chic about such a profoundly moving experience of love. Love
is not a bromide. It is a revolution. That is why chattering
about it is so absurd, cuddling up to it so silly, and a casual
approach so bizarre. Though a cause of bliss, such love can
be one of the heaviest, most painful burdens we can carry; a
charge on our whole energy, full of tension, fear and trembling, problems and claims, deepest earnest and sadness,
anxiety and suffering.

Love is rooted in the will and guided by the intellect, but
it is galvanized into heroic action and ego-annihilating union
by passionate desire. Such wild and hilarious passion is unmistakable in the lives of the saints. St. Elizabeth of Hungary's love of God was full of undaunted desire that did not
lessen her love of her husband or deprive her of the pain of
parting or the anguished longing and unappeasable loneliness
in her husband's absence. Her divine desire did not replace
her human desire. While God was consuming the great Carmelite saints of Spain and France, with unbounded desire
they continued to desire the well-being, the convivial support
and the physical presence of their family and friends. Joan of
Arc loved God but did not, because of that, love her soldiers
or her horses less. The most striking example of all is Heloise, the woman I regard as the greatest lover of all. I hope
to explain elsewhere why I think she was one of the greatest
and surest saints and mystics of all times. Here I simply want

to point out the everlasting object of her desire—Abelard. Besides being the end and the source of Heloise's longing, God was in her desire for Abelard.

Lacordaire, the famous nineteenth-century preacher of Notre Dame, said: "There are not two loves, one heavenly and the other earthly; it is but one sentiment, with the difference that the one is infinite." Long before Lacordaire, Dionysius the Areopagite, the father of Christian mysticism, intimated that there is, in the last analysis, only one love, the love that wells up eternally within the Godhead. Simon Tugwell, one of the best Dominican theologians alive today, picks up this notion and expands on it in a book on *Prayer* (Springfield, Ill.: Templegate, 1975). All created appetite, he insists, is only a partial expression of and sharing in that divine love. Our desires can only be understood in the light of God's desire—and the revelation of God in Jesus Christ legitimates such language once and for all. The harmony between God's desiring and man's is so central and acute that it is possible for God and man to be united within a single person in Jesus Christ. That hypostatic union is the type of our union with God and the most reliable indication we have of what true human desiring is.

St. John of the Cross is right to fulminate against bifurcating desires. Nevertheless, humans with their peculiar little wants do express their likeness of God; under divine guidance—and a human soul-friend would help—we must relearn how to have desires that are not disordered and contradictory, but true expressions of that love which is the life of God. The spiritual life is extremely simple. First of all we want God and then we want what he wants.

Original sin is a false grownupness, an absurd autonomy, a step-skipping, immature, and, therefore, unbearable acquisition of adult selfhood. Desire is always a reminder to us that we are not self-sufficient. Even if all I want is a piece of apple pie, which is often the case, my me, this self-made man, is already crumbling. The whole enterprise of original sin is being threatened. Obviously it is very often out of vain ambition and spiritual pride that we try to eliminate or at least inoculate desires. In the West we are more inclined to cut our desires down to a size that we can manage. And so we eke out a pretty good existence on small pleasures, but are never surprised by joy, never seduced by mystery, and never smitten by the total pleasure of God's personal, passionate Presence.

All of us, whether we know it or not, have one single desire that needs to be embodied in three developmental stages of life that can be expressed verbally with utter simplicity: *I wish / to be able / to be.* To express this desire vitally is our human vocation. The three developmental stages of growth are obvious. This chapter concentrated on the intermediate stage (*to be able*), in an effort to retrieve for this weary old world the passion and the glory of lost Christianity. If it is not retrieved, then the Church will have nothing to say to the world and no life to give to the planet.

NOTES

1. Fyodor Dostoyevsky, *Crime and Punishment,* trans. Constance Garnett (New York: Random House, Vintage Books, 1962), p. 24.
2. Aldous Huxley, *The Devils of Loudun* (New York: Harper and Row, 1979).

CHAPTER 8

The Myth of
the Great Secret

Revealed in every aspect of the universe—on all levels of existence, from the simplest material to the most advanced cosmological or most bizarre esoteric presentation of it—there is a secret. For secrecy is the fundamental epistemological category. And it can only be spoken of in myths. Those individual myths manifest the myth of the Great Secret. . . .

The mystical quest pursues a fundamental secrecy upon which the experience of consciousness rests. What the mystics meant by emptiness is what in myth is metamorphosed as the hidden knowledge the hero seeks after. Truth is ultimately secret, conveyable only through metaphors and myths which are used for speaking of ultimate truth, not because they are pretty or stylish, but because they are all one can use. The mystical statements about emptiness are not metaphysical, but epistemological.

There you have in Edwin Clark Johnson's own words a limpid and lapidary summary of his whole book, *The Myth of the Great Secret* (New York: William Morrow and Company, 1982).

Dwelling on the myth of the Great Secret is an inspired ecumenical approach. As we let go of our customary mental categories and verbal propositions, we can reflect on and browse through the cumulative traditions of humankind. Strictly speaking, there is no such thing as Hinduism, Buddhism, Taoism, Judaism, Mohammedanism, Christianity. These are all reifications of various people's dynamic, inexpressible relationships to the ultimate secret of life. Most people have, in fact, expressed the secret. But when a Buddhist expresses his relationship to the secret, it is hard enough for a fellow Buddhist to understand the meaning. How can an outsider hope to understand? And this is equally true of each of the other traditions. So we must approach each other with awesome reverence and learn as much as we can. Above all, we must love.

The best tools we have for sharing the secret knowledge are myth, metaphor and symbolic theology; in other words, mythopoeic language. The austere language of classical metaphysics has its place, but should never have been allowed to claim monopoly. Dionysius the Areopagite claims that one of the best safeguards against idolatry in the Christian tradition is the way the Bible uses seemingly inappropriate and irreverent images of God and heavenly realities. Do we get any closer to the secret by calling God truth, peace, or perfection rather than by calling him, as the Bible does, a rock, unjust judge, bed, burglar, or laundryman? The more respectable images and clear abstractions are more likely to trip us up. We are more apt to mistake these fingers pointing to the moon for the moon itself!

In his *Letters to Malcolm*, C.S. Lewis makes the point with characteristic lucidity:

> Never let us think that while anthropomorphic images are a concession to our weakness, the abstractions are the literal truth. Both are equally concessions; each singly misleading, and the two together mutually corrective. Unless you respond to it very lightly, continually murmuring, "not thus, not thus, neither is this Thou," the abstraction is fatal. It will make the life of lives in-

animate and the love of loves impersonal. The naive image is mischievous chiefly insofar as it holds unbelievers back from conversion. It does believers, even at its crudest, no harm.

Better than all our ecumenical dialogue was a Christian event celebrated in our liturgical worship annually for a thousand years. It's a long story, but the gist of it is that until the experts became too literal minded, on November 27 of every year the Church celebrated Buddha as a Christian saint. Apparently, the Church's commemoration of Buddha was quite unconscious, because when the liturgists found out that Barlaam and Josaphat were symbols of the Buddha, the feast was dropped.

I hope no one assumes that because I am tickled by the ecumenical idea of myth-making our way into the universal secret that I am also thrilled by our modern preoccupation with the esoteric. Not at all. What connects us with the secret is not the esoteric but the ascetic.

The ascetic is an uproariously happy man. He knows that God alone suffices. Although he appreciates everything and loves everyone, he is always ready to let go of everything, even his images and ideas of God—so that God himself will come and be with him, in a sense, become him. His asceticism is an effort to free himself from all that is not God. He seeks liberation from the world, the flesh and himself. He does not wage war with the world as such but with Satan's empire, the world that killed Christ, the complex network of social conventions based on and committed to the perpetuation of self-interest, self-assertion and self-aggrandizement. The flesh he abhors and combats is not his own or his neighbor's, but the body of used flesh marketed by the empire for the maintenance of a safe and soft civilization, a sybaritic waist-high culture. The self he denies is the false self, the skin-encapsulated ego, separate, alienated, loveless. He affirms his real self, the primordial, fundamental, transcendent self. But even then, he takes God so seriously (not solemnly) that he takes himself lightheartedly. In his quest for liberation, the ascetic practices poverty, chastity, and obedience so that no thing, no body, and no idea will ever impede his realized union with True Being, with Absolute Love, who exerts sovereign claim on him.

The genuine Christian attitude toward suffering seems to differ from the Buddhist attitude. True Christians know there is no way out of suffering; so they embrace it joyfully and transfigure it creatively—not looking for it, mind you, but bearing it manfully. They are also gladdened by the fact that suffering identifies them with Christ, the Suffering Servant, and are buoyed up by the knowledge that their passion leads to their resurrection, and that by filling up what is lacking to the passion of Christ they make a redemptive difference in the Third World, the Middle East, Northern Ireland, Eastern Europe, as well as their own backyard. My own experience is that only happiness that is snatched from suffering is real. All the rest is creature comfort. To live is to love; to love is to suffer. Suffering all the exigencies and challenges of life with a glad heart is the apex of asceticism. And there is no mysticism about asceticism.

When it comes to suffering, the most universal feature of the human condition, only Christ can really help. That is why Walker Percy says that the Christian should radiate an air of mystery. His very being should be redolent of other worlds, conveying an unmistakable sense of being "on to something." As a matter of fact, he is: he knows the secret—*God suffers*. As Pascal said: "Christ is in agony until the end of the world. We must not rest in the meantime." That is the distinguishing mark of Christianity.

That mark guarantees that we are riding for the brand. But it doesn't give us exclusive rights to the secret. The secret was out when the ancient Vedas were written centuries ago.

It ravished millions through *The Upanishads, The Bhagavad-Gita, The Tao-Te Ching.* The practice of Zen and Yoga initiated more and more seekers into the spellbinding secret of the One. It is hard to find a wiser statement than the central sentence of *The Bhagavad-Gita:* "He who knows the action that is in inaction, the inaction that is in action is wise indeed." The "inaction that is in action" is that "metalled appetency" that has no purpose or meaning, that chain of cause and effect that is merely driven and has no spiritual freedom. In the Oriental world this Gita gem is matched only by the center of Taoism: "The way to do is to be." Zen, too, comes to our rescue. By getting us to stand on the spot where we are and look directly at reality, it saves us from our inevitable schizophrenia and our abstract scientific tunnel vision. When we see everything in terms of space and time and number, we miss each thing's uniqueness. We miss the startling reality of "suchness" which is simply there. We all have this veil of intellection between us and reality. Enlightenment means removing this veil and finding the reality that is simply there.

I find this Oriental wisdom confirming and refreshing. But I don't find it transforming. That's neither a complaint nor a defect. It is, I believe, as it should be. My Christian and Catholic faith rejoices in and thrives on the worldwide metaphysical monstrations of God's existence and the testimony of mystics from all climes and creeds that communion with God is a well-attested human experience. I don't think Thomas Merton went far enough ecumenically. (I mention him because he made such a significant contribution to the East-West dialogue.)

Why cling stubbornly and arrogantly to that unsuitable distinction between the natural mysticism of the East and the supernatural mysticism of the West? If a person is a mystic—not merely a psychic, a spook or a self-made man but a genuine mystic—then, regardless of subject, the object, formless being, is the same. And it is supernatural. Zen *satori* and

Christian contemplation have the same direct experience of the Godhead, absolute and uncreated. If there is an experience of divine union—and that's what mysticism is all about—it must be supernatural. But the indirect and consequential inferences and interpretations differ widely.

The Christian inferences do make a world of difference, and, I dare say, a difference to the world. I personally believe that the Christian myth is the fullest expression of the truth, and when lived out in earnest, has the greatest impact on human history and the planet earth.

In the West some people—the live ones, the wise ones—sit down before facts, events, good and bad news, like little children. If they sit there long enough, growing up into adulthood without losing their childhood, taking long, leisurely, loving looks at the real; that is, learning to contemplate, then meaning will erupt out of their everyday forms of being, and their everyday minds (their body-minds, their attentive hearts) will be simply and wholly engaged. These contemplatives will become so beingful that they will overflow into the "fearful symmetry" of art or the creative and fruitful industry of work. In the West the obedient ones (*obaudire* means "to listen") are overwhelmed by One Word, which in the beginning, though divine, became flesh. The flesh was always sacred and sacramental in the West, except among those tainted and twisted by heresies. Many of us today still live under the dark cloud of Jansenism, and with shameless and unappeasable zest, we are repeating the oldest of heresies: gnosticism.

The theophanous nature of the flesh grew in the Western world and reached its peak in the body of Jesus, who became the Christ. Divine passion broke through our demonic defenses definitively in Jesus Christ who was and continues to be the fullest embodiment we have of the living God, the most lucid clue to the mystery of man. His glory is our glory. If we glory in anything else we are fools. *Orthodoxy* literally means "blazing with the right glory," not merely adhering to the right beliefs. But the right beliefs, if absorbed, assimilated, and finally transcended, do lead to and culminate in right glory, the splendor of the Godhead.

In the deepest tradition of the West, matter matters, things are cherished, events affect us profoundly, creatures link us to the Creator. But we do not merge with God or with anyone or anything else. When two drops of water merge, only one endures. All persons in heaven and on earth are indissoluble identities. We unite, we do not merge. No matter how intimate the union is—with God or with another human being—there is no dissolution of personality, no loss of identity.

If we are open to life, if we are in tune and in touch not with our descriptions of reality but with *reality* itself, then we *will* suffer, not with resignation, but with panache. And if we suffer enough, the grasping, craving, skin-encapsulated ego will die and the burgeoning Christ in us, the fundamental, transcendent self, the image and likeness of God, will emerge incandescent and indestructible. If the mystical Judaeo-Christian tradition is being tapped, then the Church can move adroitly into multiple modern worlds, into brand-new realms of consciousness; and when it does, what happens? Christ. Transformation of matter by Spirit into Christ. Evolution is his story. The only revolution with socio-political results that are permanently humanizing and therefore eternal are his story. His story equals history.

Above all else the world needs a divinely empowered, Christ-centered, worldwide revolution. That is precisely what *mystical* Christianity is. This is why, despite all the help we get from the East, so many of the journeys to the East make me sad. Something of incalculable value is lost. Turning East can be either helpful or harmful. It has been immensely beneficial to people such as Thomas Merton, Bede Griffiths, Raimundo Panikkar, David Steindl-Rast, William Irwin

Thompson, Harvey Cox, William Johnston, Richard Alpert, and Douglas Steere. The readers can probably name as many well-known women whose Christian lives were nourished by Oriental wisdom. They undoubtedly know as many people as I who became better Christ-men and Christ-women by help from Hinduism, Buddhism, Taoism, or Zen. But I also know many people who, in turning East, lost their balance and ended up unworldly indeed, but with deracinated minds and deciduous hearts.

Oriental spirituality is one of the longest and deepest traditions in the world. Countless holy men and women have grown out of that religious discipline. The wisdom of the Orient has recently begun to stimulate in the West a new appreciation for its own Judaeo-Christian heritage, its own mystical life. Thousands of religiously active—feverishly active—Westerners are starving to death spiritually because of the erosion of community and the evaporation of experience. They go through the motions of religion without becoming any more significantly related to God or his world. Their religion is bovaristic: keeping the rules and repeating the ritual, but without any religious experience, or more accurately, without any mystical experience. Western religion is not mystical enough. That is why so many people turn East.

It is almost impossible, however, for Americans to import Oriental spirituality pure and undefiled. The import ends up supporting what it was meant to undermine: the isolated, empirical, competitive ego. Instead of becoming detached from the false self, the grasping, craving ego, we become banefully detached from real persons, places, and things, leaving them behind in our quest for the newest model. Two things in particular spoil our Oriental imports: our consumer mentality and our psychidolatry. Americanized and psychologized Buddhism becomes Buddyism: casual and careless relationships because "nothing matters," irresponsibility with a spiritual veneer, a metaphysical license to avoid serious,

solemn commitments, a mystical permit to skip from one
person, bed, cause or program to another without ever taking
the plunge. The superficial merging of Oriental and Occiden-
tal spiritualities does not produce a contemplative human
being but a competitive consumer of ideas and a compulsive
devourer of experiences. We can import all the light we want
from the East but we will not become enlightened until we
become individually and collectively more human; more hu-
mane, or to put it negatively and more politically, until we
give up our personal and national quest for economic su-
premacy and military invulnerability. It is easy, even fashion-
able, to turn to the East. But to be open to the East requires
a qualitative change, a radical conversion of mind and heart,
a miracle of grace.

Since I am so tired of spiritual journeys to the Orient, or
to Guruville, California, why did I read and review at length
Johnston's psycho-Oriental book? Because the publishers sent
me the proofs and reminded me that the author and I had
met. Indeed we had, over twenty years ago. It was the mem-
ory of that meeting (history) that induced me to overcome
my antipathy toward "journey" books. I not only read this
book twice but meditated on it for weeks. (It is my conviction that if you are going to review a book you should *really*
review it.) It was the meeting that seduced me. And there's
the rub. This book is about the emptiness of everything, the
nothingness of the other and therefore the vacuity of history.
Yet it was precisely in that historical moment at precisely
that geographical location in California that two distinctly
differentiated human beings who enjoyed a unique and indestructible human existence, confronted and encountered
each other's implacable otherness in an act of holy communion. That meeting was important because something su-
premely important happened *between* us. That *exchange*
erupting at the core of every creaturely relationship is our

best clue to who God is—Love Personified, sheer altruism, the Trinity.

One wholesome feature that I look forward to as a result of the ongoing communion between East and West is a unifying, inclusive reply to the crucial question: Is all *real living* altered states of higher consciousness or is it "meeting"? Any normal, integrated—though, of course, imperfect person should, I believe, experience the twofold tug in his or her life. The "concentration without elimination" attained through recollection or through a no-nonsense practice of Zen or Yoga or any art of self-mastery should ready one for an incomparably richer experience of presence in every meeting. And then the final question, it seems to me, would be concerned not with the degree of consciousness but the quality of responses. They are, once again, related aspects of one life. But which is the end?

Much of today's preoccupation with altered states of consciousness has far more to do with the isolated exaltation of man than with the adoration of God. One of the interesting things that electroencephalography has demonstrated is that the human brain puts out at least four kinds of electrical currents, referred to by researchers as alpha, beta, delta, and theta waves. Theta waves are the exciting ones. Technicians believe that these are the waves that account for the visions of the great mystics and for the focused attention of people who have practiced meditation for years. As a result of this research, the investigators are convinced that what took the saintly ascetic three years to accomplish can now be attained in three weeks. This simple device has lured many people away from the arduous following of Christ. Consequently, pseudomystics abound. Letting technique dominate religious experience is comparable to attributing an uproariously happy marriage of twenty-five years to sexual technique. Anyone who is serious about man or God, *moksha* or *satori*, will not see in

those wavy lines any evidence for what or whom he is passionately seeking. Throughout human history the result of
technique has not been a heightening but rather a narrowing
and flattening of human experience. Eric Gill's poignant cry
still rings in the air: "Good Lord, the thing was a mystery
and we tried to measure it."

THE ART OF CONTEMPLATION

The narcissist is a miserable contemplative. He contem-
plates himself in a kind of mystical masturbation. That makes
him miserable, since it is impossible to enjoy yourself while
you contemplate yourself. In other words, the enjoyment and
the contemplation of our inner activities are incompatible.
When you see a sunset, you enjoy the act of seeing and contemplate the sunset. When you touch a perfect body, you
enjoy the feeling and contemplate the body. Later on, if you
analyze the sense of touch or scrutinize your feeling, you are
then contemplating the feeling and enjoying the thought. In
the wake of your beloved's death, you contemplate the death
and enjoy the grief. If you grieve too long, your friends begin
to worry and so they contemplate your loneliness and enjoy
their anxiety.

If you look at your faith, you stop believing at that moment; if you look at your love, you stop loving; if you look
at your hope, you stop hoping. You interrupt these God-centered acts by turning around to look at them. Once you squint
back to see how you are contemplating, you cease to contemplate—or you change the object of your contemplation. The
surest way to spoil a meal or an encounter is to start examining your satisfaction. All introspection is to some degree
short-circuited: we try to look inside ourselves to see what is
going on, but the moment we look, it stops. Instead we find
mental images and physical sensations. C.S. Lewis writes
about all this in *Surprised by Joy*. "The great error," he says,

"is to mistake this mere sediment or track or by-product for the activities themselves." Not that these activities, before we stopped them, were unconscious. Lewis says that we need more than the twofold division into conscious and unconscious. We need a threefold division: the unconscious, the enjoyed, and the contemplated.

Most contemplative efforts in our narcissistic age are futile attempts to contemplate the enjoyed. We are determined to capture joy, so we swallow pills, take injections, consume alcohol, exploit others, go on trips, reveal our naked bodies, and bare our souls; we prowl around the sanctuary of our psyches looking for high experiences; and all that we find is either an image or a quiver in the diaphragm, "a mental track left by the passage of joy, and not the wave but the wave's imprint on the sand."

Hopefully, it is now ineluctably clear that the nub of the art of contemplation is artlessness or naiveté. There is no method or formal technique for realizing union with God. To realize union is a very simple and childlike affair. We complicate the whole business by our egotistic compulsion to achieve, to attain, and to accomplish. Did not Jesus say that his yoke is easy and his burden light? (Matt. 11:30) Meister Eckhart put it best:

> He who fondly imagines to get more of God in thoughts, prayers, pious offices and so forth, than by the fireside or in the stall: in sooth he does but take God, as it were, and swaddle his head in a cloak and hide him under the table. For he who seeks God under settled forms lays hold of the form while missing the God concealed in it. But he who seeks God in no special guise lays hold of him as he is in himself, and such a one "lives with the Son" and is the life itself.

We become ingenuous, less rigid and self-conscious when we recognize God as the active agent of our spiritual lives.

He loves, hounds, woos, holds, and captivates us. All we can do is respond. Realization comes and the possessive will surrenders itself when we feel spiritually bankrupt and are thoroughly convinced that struggle and squirm as we may, there is no escape from the love of God.

Being gratefully receptive and keenly responsive is a far cry from the nullity of quietism. Eschewing or at least minimizing contemplative methods and techniques is meant in no way to repudiate a balanced asceticism or a discipline of life, but to avoid any kind of rigid methodology. It is just such a methodology that, in our own day, has been turned into a pharmacology of mysticism—"mist-to-schism" freaks swallowing pills and turning on.

The only way you can possess God is to be possessed by him. The only way to enjoy him is to let him go. The only way to be heightened is to be humbled. The only way into the light of day is through the darkness of night. The only way to be divinely enriched is to be so poor you don't even have a god. God, through the work of his hands, his creation, takes hold of us; not the other way round. Our grasping, acquisitive nature spoils things. The beauty you leap upon dissolves under your dead weight. Clutch the splendor of flame and you get burned; pluck a flower and it dies; scoop water from a brook and it flows no longer; snatch the wind in a bag and you have dead air. The more bloody determined you are to capture life and hold on to it, the more life will elude you and your own self-asserting effort imprison you. To enjoy any living thing—fire, water, air, animal, vegetable, human, God himself—we must let go of it. When we free it from our grasp, we, too, become free. In detachment is our liberation; and in our liberation the earth is hallowed and God is glorified.

Divine union is realized not by programs and practices cleverly devised or solemnly prescribed and religiously adhered to, but by a life of creative fidelity lived fully without bargaining, compromising, or holding back. In other words, realization of union with God is the graceful result of authentic human experience: life, deeply participated in and intelligently interpreted.

The rhythm of religious experience is made up of an awareness and a processive affirmation that are interconnected: we first become aware of the given relationship, which comes from creation itself and from God's initiative within us. Then we affirm this relationship, accept it personally with gratitude. When we will it, we are renewed, deepened, and transposed to a new level—from the ontological to the spiritual. We are led to communion with God, not as a merely natural being, but as a personal being. It is through this intimate and existential claim or passionate affirmation (the willingness to suffer life) that the given-ness of union with God becomes interiorized and personalized. This is necessarily so, since man is not only a ravished recipient of cosmic disclosures but a passionate pilgrim of the Absolute.

We are all indissoluble touchstones of reality. No reality (even God) is independent of touchstones; but neither is there any "touch" independent of contact with an Otherness that transcends my own subjectivity even when I respond to it from the subjective ground of my being and know it only in my contact with it. Events and meetings that are mindful and contemplative enough constitute the world of spirituality, the matrix of mysticism. A way into the present and the future opens up for us not in the philliloo but in the silent and solitary residue of these events and meetings. For these residues I claim what cannot be claimed for any objective metaphysics or subjective inspiration. They are "touchstones of reality." Today we aren't in need of theological systems or linguistic analyses or a plethora of "experiences," but "an opening way."

The touchy-feely, hootchy-cootchy craze that captivated our national fantasy a couple of decades ago made a certain contribution insofar as it punctured our puritanical inhibitions in certain tactile—often tacky—ways. But very quickly it fell into its own homemade trap. We became enthralled by the new experience of touching. St. Elizabeth of Hungary and St. Francis of Assisi, ardent followers of Christ, went through the touchy-feely stage too, but they went after lepers! Our penchant was for the "beautiful people," the nubile nymph or the handsome hulk.

What the "touchers" learned, I hope, is that to touch is to go through and *beyond* subjective experiencing: if you and I touch, then there is communication that is neither merely objective nor merely subjective nor both together. The very act of touching is already a transcending of the self in openness to the impact of something other than the self. When two people really touch each other as persons—physically or not—the touching is not merely a one-sided impact: it is a mutual revelation of two solitaries.

If I have touchstones, then I don't need to cling possessively and fractiously to iron-clad systems and ideologies that supposedly contain either universal meaning or a meaning that is merely subjective and cultural. All I need is a touchstone of reality. On that stone all I have to do is to be, to simply "look at the lilies of the field" (Matt. 7:28) with no designs on them. From that touchstone I can see things as they really are. Standing still on that piece of reality, I can let the dread of the past and the fear of the future fall away from me while I gaze as lovingly and directly as I can on whatever is present.

To wizened Westerners who seem finished, fastened as they so often are to the fixtures of religion rather than to the ineffable Godhead, I highly recommend the wisdom of the East. It is bound to break through our crusty old ways of thinking, our inordinate attachment to words, images, and ideas, however sacred, our fear of the emptiness that lies just below the exciting surface of things, and provide a guiding light, an opening way toward Reality.

The Oriental way, however, needs to be critically assessed, for I do not believe that all ways are equal. There are countless touchstones, some better than others. There are numerous myths, some richer than others. But ultimately there is one way, and it is not a doctrine or a teaching or a technique or a system of beliefs, but a personal, passionate exchange going on at the "still point of the turning world." This is the secret: the sacrificial love that creates or (in our case) co-creates the inner (and *outer*) suchness of things. The funny thing about the Christian Myth is that God could not keep the secret. The telling of it was the Word, and the Word became flesh. And so Christ said, "I am the Way" (John 14:6).

The true Christian mystic never outgrows an absolute need for the mediation of Christ. On the one hand, as George Tavard points out in *Theological Studies* (December 1981), John of the Cross supported new views of the Incarnation, as in *Romances* 1–9: the purpose of creation is to provide a bride whom the Son of God will espouse in the Incarnation. On the other hand, the sixteenth-century Carmelite doctor was more emphatic than anyone else that Jesus Christ is the one, only, and total Word of the Father, after whose coming the Father has nothing to add.

"Man cannot bear too much reality." No one knew this better than Prince Siddhartha Gautama. According to the Buddha legend, he left his wife and child and devised a way to "nirvana," to "nonexistence," so there would be no suffering.

Naturally, he has a large following in America, especially among those who believe in the American dream and the pursuit of happiness. All the psychological professions are drawn to this way since their business is to normalize and

tranquillize people and lessen the pain of life. The trouble
with this comfortable procedure is that you end up with a lot
of happy zombies instead of heroic saints. There is a famous
Buddhist metaphor emphasizing detachment: "If on the way
you meet the Buddha, kill him." Even as a metaphor this
seems too violent. May I suggest a more gentle approach? "If
on the way you meet the Buddha, wipe that smile off his
face."

Much of the teaching of the East and the apophatic theology of the West exaggerates the negative dimension. It is
much healthier, holier, and far more realistic to live acutely
and wittily in the creative tension between "thou art that"
and "thou art not that." We must distinguish mere nothingness from the sense of nothingness. To think of ourselves as
nothing leads to feckless folly or despair. To be haunted by
a sense of nothingness leads to holiness. We are *relatively*
nothing—nothing apart from God, nothing except insofar as
we are known, loved, and sustained in being by God's creative act. Our existence is fragile and contingent; we are next
to nothing. If God ceased to uphold us for one moment, we
would disintegrate. Sister Elizabeth of the Trinity, a French
Carmelite mystic, went so far as to define mystical prayer as
"the meeting of Him who is with her who is not." Our sense
of nothingness is so trenchant that our need for the Absolute
is absolute. Our search grows out of a personal need for a
person whose mercy and tenderness extends to the weakest
and farthest depths of creation. The secret is Love, not emptiness, not meaninglessness, but a love so unbounded and
limitless that it evokes from the imperfect, or rather, unfin-
ished lover an eerie sense of the void. St. John the Evangelist
said God is love (I John 4:16). St. Augustine went even further and said love is God.

CHAPTER 9

From Solitude to Storytelling

Christ called himself the temple (cf. John 2:20–21), and at that crucial historical moment he shifted the axis of the whole world from buildings, cities, and even the home as the center that holds people together, and replaced that center with something extremely personal and indispensable for mediating between estranged humanity and the ineffable Godhead: himself. As God-man he is the mediator. He is, by nature, in essence, *priest*.

When Jesus urged the fishermen to follow him, promising to make them fishers of men, he subsequently actualized that promise of the most essential ministry by sharing with them his own priestly powers. They would be priests indeed: celebrating sacramentally what God has done and continues to do in Christ, and with scorched lips and broken hearts not only preaching the Word of God but vitally embodying it. If they do not embody it, they will die. If they do embody it, they will be killed. There is no other way to be priest.

Then Jesus instituted the Church, not to organize religion, but to personalize it: to keep the personal passionate Presence of God alive forever at the creative center of all human affairs. Through baptism we immerse ourselves in the life of the Church and are Christened a priestly people.

What can we do in this modern world, which will not transcend itself, which has lost touch with the sacred, with its center and its source of life? Temple, church and palace have been abolished or banalized. Everything has been profaned, that is, thrust outside the sphere of the holy. Sacred mountains and groves are gone. The world of man and nature is emptied of transcendent significance, of any ultimate meaning. No wonder there is a rebellion among the young against the drab, one-dimensional world. Hordes of them travel to India to discover the sense of the sacred, the inner meaning of life which has been lost in the West. But, as Dom Bede Griffiths, O.S.B. sadly reassures us, India, too, is rapidly losing it.

Wherever modern civilization spreads, all holiness, all sense of the sacred, all sense of transcendent reality disappears. This decline of the West and diminution of the Spirit in the East is another dramatic Fall of Man. What can we do in the face of our narcissistic culture and in the path of the techno-barbaric juggernaut? We can become high priests of creation by participation in the high priesthood of Jesus.

As high priests we must always be passionate. Passion literally means "to be abandoned." That is the central, final human stance: positive, creative abandonment to God. Human glory will not be achieved by answering topical questions such as "What does modern man need?" What needs to be answered first is the dominical question: "What does God require of you?" And this can only be answered existentially by passionate surrender. By annealing passion, the high priest becomes a Christ-man or a Christ-woman.

Based on the requirements of God conveyed to us through Scripture and tradition and the needs of contemporary society, requirements obvious to anyone awake enough to perceive them, there are seven qualities that ought to be unmistakable marks of any genuine high priest of creation who is always engaged in *contemplative* action. (In a balanced society I would have emphasized both words, *contemplative* and *action*, but since our society is convulsed by feverish and uninspired activities, I need to emphasize the one ingredient that validates and enriches action and makes its results enduringly effective, and that is contemplation.) Through no alliterative contrivance on my part, these seven hard-won virtues all begin with the same letter—"s." How felicitous. It will help you remember the seven marks of the Christian high priest.

SOLITUDE

The high priest should be solitary. Why? Primarily because of the enthralling nature of God. The high priest of creation belongs to God. Like Jesus himself, he cannot be defined primarily by his work. What Jesus did was of secondary importance. Who he was was primary. Dietrich Bonhoeffer misinterpreted Christ's position. Jesus was not "the man for others." Essentially he was the *man from the Other*, the Wholly Other. His altruistic ministry was an opulent, lavish overflow of his fullness of being. He was a desert man, a solitary, who came out of hiding late in life, walked into the marketplace and left that motley, muddled gaggle of humanity utterly transfigured.

Three times Jesus asked Peter if he loved him. When he was sure that Peter really did, then he commissioned him to feed his flock (John 21:15–17). Loving one another is a proof of the love of God. But so is wasting time with the Beloved. If a Christian skips that kind of holy leisure, spousal prayer, then his service in the community is not a self-sacrificing act of love. It is just another job by another man in the profession who is fulfilling his own needs.

The only communities I know worth their salt are communities of solitaries. I don't mean cavemen, bucolic old coots, Wordsworthian wonder-wowers, or any of the enormously popular and corpulent breed of modern omphalopsychites (navel-gazers). I mean persons who are so rooted and centered, so in touch and in tune with the infinite and inexhaustible ground of their being, that their being-fulness over-flows, they share what they contemplate—and community occurs.

The solitary is not a lonely person; he is undividedly engaged. He has not withdrawn, he is summoned, and he is there. He is not wasting his talents, he is being squandered by life. He is not idling, he is biding his time. God does not act in a vacuum. He needs human instrumentality. The solitary is always there—available, vulnerable, ready to be sent.

That is why the Christian high priest cannot be "one of the gang." He must be eagerly disposed, discreetly available, full of compassion, but never a victim of the crowd. It is not his organizing energies, his gregarious talents, his frenzied activities that put him in touch with the community. It is his deep relationship with God who asserts daily his sovereign claim on him. God is not satisfied with our work. He wants the whole person directly and immediately—all to himself—*at least* one whole day a week and one hour a day for both communal liturgy and solitary spousal prayer. (Since Sunday is a service day for ordained priests and catechists, they must pick another day to be with God alone.) The person who is not a solitary is either a fop, a foozel or a spiritual robot.

Not only God himself, but others demand that we be solitary. Our ability to serve properly depends entirely upon our inescapable role as *paranymph*. In Greek antiquity the para-nymph was the one who went to fetch the bridegroom. The high priest should often be mysteriously missing. Where is he? Not on the golf course, in Florida, in bed, or at another meeting; but gone to fetch the bridegroom! That's the thrilling secret Christians are on to. If they are not obviously, tremulously on to it, they are perilously off the wall! If the bridegroom is not fetched, the people are betrayed by those who have become parasites instead of paranymphs.

SOLIDARITY

The discreet solitude of any high priest is a creative protest against the euphoric or chaotic togetherness that stamps our way of life in the modern world. But it is also the highest and most apt expression of our solidarity with the whole human race, with the whole of creation. The more solitary we are, the more divinely endowed and psychologically equipped to enter into a significantly profound relationship with all levels of life—animal, vegetable and mineral as well as human—affirming and consecrating our solidarity with all being.

SUFFERING

Neither joy nor sorrow escapes the high priest of creation. He is "a man for all seasons," in touch with all creatures who both reveal and veil God. High priests cannot shun anyone or anything. Their pastoral care, for instance, cannot merely include the people in their domain but must extend to the animals, trees, flowers, parks, ponds, air, buildings, etc. Every high priest is marked as an *alter-Christus*. If we are to identify with Christ, the high priest of creation, and the willful leonine victim of love, then we must freely decide to suffer all of life. Such a radical choice designates with unmistakable clarity and poignancy our inevitable end: we will be crucified. But we will also rise jubilantly from the dead: our horizons will be infinitely broadened, the quality of our life hilariously enhanced.

SWEETNESS

Ordinarily I am repelled by the word *sweet*. But deep below its hackneyed, commonplace use there is a proper meaning so rollicking and robust that I must resort to it now to

counteract what might seem too grim and solemn a description of the Christian life. Every high priest should be sweet
in the deepest sense of that word. Without forfeiting one whit
of our prophetic fury and moral outrage, we should be, like
our Master, gentle, tender, compassionate, and intuitive. Like
Jesus, yes, but also like a good woman. We all need a strong
anima. In every one of us—man as well as woman—the fem-
inine principle must be keenly developed and highly refined.
This will not emasculate us, but make us more manly ("vir-
tuous" and "virile") than ever. Until American men discover
the internal woman and integrate this dark, soft, receptive,
mysterious part of themselves into their total personality, they
cannot be persons of prayer, high priests, or apostles. How
can we bear Christ into the world without becoming Marian
to the core?

SILENCE

The high priest of creation is silent. Most of the world's
great religious leaders, in ancient as well as in modern times,
are men or women who keep silent most of the time. The
outstanding examples of both East and West remain speech-
less for most of their lives. Yet they have a prodigiously active
influence on the world. One of the greatest religious leaders
of all time said: "He who speaks doesn't know and he who
knows doesn't speak." The secular leader also needs silence.
Charles de Gaulle knew this, as did Mahatma Gandhi and
Dag Hammarskjold. That is one reason why they were effective leaders.

You may object: silence is for monks. And you would be
absolutely wrong. The monk does not own silence. Silence is
the property of every man, woman and child. It is a human
value. The monk simply accentuates, weds, and witnesses to
this rich and silent dimension of life so that it will not be lost
or forgotten in the talkative turmoil of everyday life. Only if

we speak rarely and with discretion can we speak with any authority at all. Otherwise we are not worth hearing.

If I knew a renowned orator, an eloquent preacher, who talked all day long on the phone, on the job, on the street, and then jumped like a hot shot from a veritable vesuvius of loquacity into the pulpit, I would not want to listen to him. We have no right to talk more than we listen. We should be listening most of the time, night and day, to the Word, the second person of the Blessed Trinity. St. John of the Cross said that from all eternity God speaks one Word. That Word reached its fullness in Christ. Nothing remains to be said. But think of all the silence needed to attend to, digest, and assimilate the Word made flesh: "To whom shall we go? You alone have the words of eternal life" (John 6:68).

The Word was made flesh. All flesh embodies him. How absorbed can one finite creature be? There is first of all the omnipresence of God—God participating in all of creation, sustaining, strengthening and renewing us, making all things new. Then the passion of God breaks through definitively and God becomes man, the high priest of creation. Jesus becomes the Christ. We surely have spotted the Logos and have God focused insofar as we take time to contemplate in silence the historical, mystical, and cosmic Christ. If we cannot pray, we are gagged; if we cannot kneel, we are fettered; if we cannot be quiet, we are a nuisance. We may be popular momentarily, but the frenetic ferrago we offer is fruitless in the long run.

STORYTELLING

The high priest of creation is a storyteller—mythical and mystical. The truth is much too large and inscrutable to be contained inside of neat, tidy, categorical concepts and ideas. Doctrine and theology are indispensable, but they are not enough. The faith did not initially come to us as systematic theology. It came as story. Tell me about God: "Once upon a time there was a garden. . . ." Tell me about Jesus: "Once upon a time there was a boy in a little town in Palestine called Nazareth. . . ." Tell me about salvation: "When that same boy grew up, he loved people so much that the rulers began to get frightened of him, and do you know what they did? . . ." Tell me about the Church: "A group of people, including his mother, took this man very seriously, identified themselves with him and kept his spirit alive, and do you know what happened to them? . . ."

The story faded and monumental doctrinal theses developed. In losing the story we have lost both the power and the glory. What Hilaire Belloc said seems irrefutable: "Truth must always be clothed in splendor." We have committed the unpardonable sin of transforming exciting stories into dull systems. We must recover the story if we are to recover a faith for our day. We must tell and retell the old, old story and in the telling of it discover and discern our own story, our own experience of God. To tell the Bible story is to move from myth to mysticism, from marvels to meaning, from eros to agape, from events to experience.

Jews in Eastern Europe in the eighteenth century were in trouble, and when times were extremely harsh the Baal Shem Tov would take himself off to a particular part of the forest to meditate and pray. He would first light a fire, then recite a special prayer. After this, the danger or misfortune facing the struggling little Jewish community would be averted. There would be a miracle.

The Baal Shem's disciple, the Maggid of Mezeritch, tried to maintain this tradition after the master's death. When disaster struck the community, he, too, would go into the forest and find the spot where his master prayed. He was not, however, completely familiar with the ritual practiced by the Baal Shem. All he could say was, "Lord of the Universe, hear me! I know nothing about lighting the fire. All I can do is say the prayer." It was enough. The disaster was averted and the little community lived in peace.

Later on it fell to Moseh-Leib of Sassov to bear responsibility for the people. When tragedy threatened, he, too, would go into the forest and simply say, "Alas, I do not know the prayer. At least I know the place. This is the best I can do." Again the miracle happened and the people were saved.

Finally the burden fell on the shoulders of Israel of Rizhin. When misfortune struck, all he could do was sit in his chair with his head in his hands. He addressed God in this way: "O Lord, I cannot light the fire and I have no idea about the prayer. Even the place is hidden from me. The best I can do is tell the story. This will have to do." The mere telling of the story was enough to avert misfortune.

To keep faith and love alive and in the end to overcome death, we must keep telling the greatest story every told, the Christ-story.

But—and this is the clincher—as pioneers and pilgrims of the Absolute, we must not depend too much on the story, on the map, on what is known, safe and familiar. Dependency would kill us, for it is the unknown that gives us life. The unknown flowers when we are receptive to it and allow it to enter. The unknown carries us to the constantly forming edge of the world where light, beauty and ecstasy are found. There is no other path to the spiritual, to the creative, to the real.

There is a story about being storier than is good for you. A woman came to Rabbi Israel, the Maggid of Koznitz, and told him with many tears that she had been married a dozen years and still had not borne a son. "What are you willing to do about it?" he asked her. She did not know what to say. "My mother," the Maggid told her, "was aging and still had no child. Then she heard that the Holy Baal Shem was stopping over in Apt in the course of a journey. She hurried to his inn and begged him to pray she might bear a son. 'What are you willing to do about it?' he asked. 'My husband is a poor bookbinder,' she replied, 'but I do have one fine thing that I shall give to the Rabbi.' She went home as fast as she could and fetched her good cape, her 'katinka,' which was carefully stored away in a chest.

"But when she returned to the inn with it, she heard that the Baal Shem had already left for Mezbizh. She immediately set out after him and since she had no money to ride, she walked from town to town with her 'katinka' until she came to Mezbizh. The Baal Shem took the cape and hung it on the wall. 'It is well,' he said. My mother walked all the way back, from town to town, until she reached Apt. A year later I was born."

"I, too," cried the woman to the Maggid, "will bring you a good cape of mine, so that I may get a son." "That won't work," said the Maggid. "You heard the story. My mother had no story to go by." [1]

We must have such courageous trust in life that discreetly and awesomely but unflinchingly we move into the unknown, unmapped and unstoried Abyss of pure faith, into the luminous darkness of the Hidden God. And who knows if we will come out alive?

SHARING OF THE GOOD NEWS

The Gospel is bad news before it is good news: the sinfulness of man and consequently what man has done to man, but then the redemption, the resurrection and the victorious centrality of the love of God, a love that sustains, strengthens, and renews us forever.

It is challenge enough to hold our peace in a world of verbosity. Perhaps the toughest challenge of all, in a worldwide, respectable atmosphere of mendacity, is to tell the truth. Our age resembles the catastrophic end of Shakespeare's *King Lear*. The stage is covered with corpses and only Edgar is left. He stammers: "The weight of this sad time we must obey/Speak what we feel, not what we ought to say."

Like Shakespeare, Christian high priests must tell the truth. There is hardly anything more crucial for us than to obey the sadness of our times by taking it into account without equivocation or subterfuge, by speaking out of our times and into our times not merely what we ought to say about the Gospel, not merely what it would appear to be in the interests of the Gospel for us to say, but what we ourselves have felt about it. Whatever the risk, we must preach the Gospel truth, the truth we ourselves must live by. If we are faithful to the truth, our lives will be torn by tragedy, healed by comedy, and delightfully revolutionized by one serendipity after another.

Even when we share the good news, our silence must be shattering. Better to leave others dumbstruck at the brink of mystery, awed by unspeakable Glory, than well informed but snug and secure. Before it is a word, the Gospel that is truth is silence, a pregnant silence in its ninth month. In answer to Pilate's question, "What is truth?" Jesus keeps silent (John 19:38). Even with his hands tied behind him, he manages somehow to hold silence out like a terrible gift.

When the Pharisees tried to get Jesus to quell the glorious hoopla that swelled sonorously all around him while he rode his orgulous mule into the city, the meek and mighty man from Nazareth simply said: "I tell you, if these were silent, the very stones would cry out" (Luke 19:40). The point is, of course, that the stones do cry out. Not only the stones, but the rivers and the hills, the animals, the children, the workers, the old folks, the refugees, the Cubans, the Africans, the Tibetans, the Indians, the Blacks, the Eskimos, the Russians, the Americans, the Slavs, the Chinese and Japanese, the Vietnamese, Cambodians and Koreans, the Arabs, Jews and Europeans. They all cry out truth, and their cry is poignant, salient and devastating.

Before the Gospel is good or bad news, it is simply the news that "that's the way it is," any day, any year. Quell the multifarious forms of newzak and muzak and the silence of the stones will cry out like thunder! We must be led beyond the words, songs, and ceremonies into silence, into mystery, into the consuming fire of God's love.

In the early days of the Church, a young man went to his teacher and said: "Father, according as I am able, I keep my little fast, my prayer, meditation, and contemplative silence; and according as I am able, I strive to cleanse my heart of thoughts. Now, what more should I do?" The old man rose up in reply and stretched out his hands to heaven, and his fingers became like ten lamps of fire. He said, "Why not be totally changed into fire?"

The Christian high priest of creation must be like this: totally turned into fire. The fierce and fiery representatives of God don't last long: they burn out quickly. Jesus said, "I have come to cast fire on the earth, and how I wish it were blazing already" (Luke 12:49). We must live so passionately that we are not merely warmed by the fire that Christ came into the world to ignite but utterly devoured by it.

NOTES

1. Elie Wiesel, *The Gates of the Forest* (New York: Holt, Rinehart and Winston, 1966).